ADVENTURE
TRAIL

ADVENTURE TRAIL

Eve Harlow
and
Peter Foxwell

LUTTERWORTH PRESS
Richard Smart Publishing

First published 1978

Published by Lutterworth Press
Luke House, Farnham Road, Guildford, Surrey
and Richard Smart Publishing

Copyright © Eve Harlow and Peter Foxwell, 1978
ISBN 0 7188 7018 2
Printed by John G. Eccles Printers Ltd., Inverness

Contents

Foreword

At the end of this year, groups of young people aged between 17 and 24 years will be starting out on an adventure of a lifetime. They will be joining Operation Drake, the great round-the-world expedition, using a 150-ton sailing ship as a floating base for a series of important expeditions in the tropics. Of course, there will be sailors, soldiers and airmen who have experience of expeditions to guide them, but the young explorers, as we call them, will be playing a leading part in the tasks.

We shall start out from Plymouth and will be anchoring in exciting places such as Panama and Papua-New Guinea. I am sure you wish that you were coming too. I wish you were — but it is only possible for us to involve 216 young explorers during the two-year voyage.

All the young men and women who are joining us on this venture are being carefully chosen from thousands who have applied. They were recommended by their schools, clubs, companies, cadet forces and Army Regiments. Choosing the final crew was very hard indeed — almost impossible, in fact, because everyone of the youngsters recommended to me was special in some way. Some had done navigation, which is going to be very useful. Others knew something about handling sailing boats. But they all had one thing in common; they had a spirit of adventure, a willingness to go out into the world and find out about other lands and peoples, and help others. They also had a personal courage and confidence that comes from knowing yourself, and knowing what you are capable of achieving. Many boys and girls have the spark of adventure in them. I

imagine you must have it or you would not be
reading this book.

Being courageous is an admirable quality,
and many of the famous adventurers have been
very brave. But there is more to being an explorer.
Discipline and common sense are important too.
They are essential qualities. On most expeditions
everyone's life will depend on discipline at some
point. When the leader gives an order he or she
has to be sure that it will be carried out instantly.
On a ship the order may be something which has
to be done quickly to combat the sea or a change
in the wind. This is why we believe it is so
important in the Armed Forces. Discipline means
self-discipline too — doing jobs which are tiring or
unpleasant, but doing them just as well as you can
nevertheless.

Being a good team member is the other
essential for an adventurer. There are times when
someone goes off on his own, and his courage,
self-discipline and common sense will keep him
safe. But if there are more than two of you, then
you should work together as a team, each helping
the other, each doing his part for the good of the
team.

This book, *Adventure Trail*, is for boys and
girls who have a feeling for adventure. It will show
you ways in which you can enjoy yourself in the
open air and start getting ready for more
ambitious adventures when you are older. It will
also help you to understand the countryside and
the animals that live in it. You will learn
something about camping and looking after
yourself away from towns and shops. There is
something about map reading and finding your

way across open country. In fact, I have learned quite a lot myself from the book.

Perhaps after reading it you will want to learn more about adventure. There are clubs and associations you can join: some of them are listed at the end of the book. If you start getting yourself ready now perhaps, in a few years, you will be able to voyage in a large sailing ship, or explore a great river, or cross a desert. Don't think that all this world has been explored because it hasn't, and there is a great deal of scientific exploration still to be done.

As long as you are not afraid of hard work or getting your hands dirty; if you have enterprise and initiative, plus an enquiring mind and a taste for adventure, then the great outdoors is yours to explore, and enjoy. May I wish you all the best of luck and hope you keep up the Outward Bound tradition.

April 1978   *John Blashford-Snell*
                               Lt.Col., Royal Engineers

Going on
the adventure trail

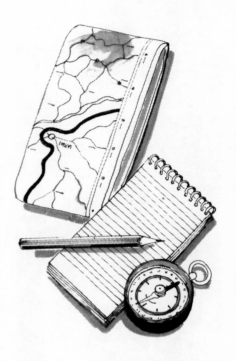

When the next long, summer holiday starts, get together with two or three friends and plan a journey. This is a marvellous way of getting out of the house, and seeing somewhere new. It is the best way of spending time with your friends. Do not think of it simply as a day together 'mucking about'. Make it a real journey, with a purpose and a plan. Decide on somewhere that you all want to visit. A place you have never been to before. It might be a lake, or a park. It might be a forest or a river. It could even be a small town you have never visited. There will be some adventure in the journey, you can be sure of that. No matter where you go, something exciting, or interesting, or funny, will happen on the way. If you are fairly young, you can go on a day's journey. If you are older, you might decide to spend a night away, camping — or even a weekend. You know best how long you can be away. If you have the kind of parents who have encouraged you to get out and about, then they will be interested in your plans. Discuss it with them before you get down to the real planning with your friends.

A lot of the fun in a journey is in the planning. Get out the map. Study it. Discuss the route and how far you have to travel, there and back. Read anything you can about the place you want to see. And if you have outdoor hobbies or interests, see if the journey can include them. One person should be expedition leader. As you grow older, you will find that there are people who get things going. There are also people who fall in with other people's plans. If you are one of the people who like to start things, you are probably going to be leader of your expedition!

Expedition planning

On a big expedition, such as an assault on a mountain or the navigation of a big river, there is always a team leader. He chooses the rest of the team. Everyone on the team has a special job to do in the planning. One may do the research, reading up everything that has been written about the place and making a report to the team leader. He would find out about the type of country the expedition would be travelling through and what kind of weather they could expect. The ways and customs of the native people would be important. It might be necessary for some of the team to learn a local dialect.

Someone else would be given the job of ordering and buying the food for the expedition. How much should they take with them and how much could they buy locally? What kinds of food would be needed so that everyone stayed healthy and no-one got bored with the menus.

Another member of the team would look after the equipment, cameras, radios, tents, trucks and so on. There is usually a doctor on the team of a big expedition. He plans medicines and equipment for treating the kinds of illnesses that the team might get during the expedition.

The team leader gets all the information from his team and with it he plans the transporting so that everything and everyone gets to the starting place on time. He can also decide how many porters he needs to carry supplies. When the expedition actually begins, the team leader uses his men and equipment in the way that makes a successful job of the trip.

This kind of planning has a special word — logistics. Logistics actually means the moving and quartering of troops. Explorers and expedition leaders use the word to describe the planning of moving men, equipment and supplies from place to place.

Elect a leader
Your journey is obviously not going to need detailed planning like this. But it does help to have a leader on a trek. If there are only two of you, it is fairly easy for one to say 'you build the fire and I will get some water'. Three or more, and you need a team leader so that everything gets done and no one feels left out. Four people, incidentally, is the least number you should have if you are going on a trek into open country. Then, if anyone gets hurt, two can go for help, travelling together while one stays with the injured person.

How far to go
If walking is a new idea to you, the first thing you should decide is how far you want to go. On average, a young person can walk about 2 miles in an hour. A man can walk 4 miles an hour easily. On your map, draw a circle round your home of about 2 miles radius. The scale of the map will tell you how big the circle should be. (See page 19 for Map Scales and Distance). Study the area inside the circle and see if there is anywhere that you would like to visit. Perhaps there is a lake or a river you have never seen. Or a hill you have never climbed. Perhaps there is a town which you can explore?
You will have to walk two miles to get to your destination and two miles back. 4 miles altogether. You should be able to do this on your first walk without too much difficulty. One or two walks like this and you should be able to go further. 6 miles in a day should not be too much for a young person. On a bicycle of course, you can do more miles.

Walking

Walking boots are made of leather and have a ridged sole

You have planned your route on the map and you have worked out how many miles you are going to walk. That is, if you keep to the main roads or paths. You might decide to go off down an unmarked lane or across an area of open country. As long as you have your map and a compass, and you are wearing a watch, you should be perfectly alright. Indeed, part of the fun of walking is being able to make detours. It is not quite so easily done if you are cycling. You usually have to keep to the roads!

Be comfortable
What are you going to wear for walking? Long trousers are best, for both boys and girls. Denim jeans are ideal for ordinary conditions. Denim is fairly windproof and if the jeans are not too new, they can be comfortable to wear. Do not buy your jeans so that they fit too tightly. You may think they look smarter but, after two or three hours walking, a tight pair of jeans is going to chafe the skin in your crutch and behind your knees. Choose a straight-leg style and one that fits neatly round the waist rather than hipsters. On a warm day, wear a cotton vest or a T-shirt with a sleeved shirt over the top. Have a lightweight sweater to wear in the early morning and evening when it is cooler.

A windcheater is the best kind of top garment and on cold days, you would probably want to wear woollen mitts or gloves and a knitted hat or cap.

Are those shoes for walking?
If you are like most young people, you spend your life wearing sneakers, sandals or some other kind of casual footwear. Girls sometimes wear knee boots and some boys like fashionable, soft, suede-surfaced

'desert boots'. None of these is of any use for
walking. If you are going to get any fun at all out
of adventuring into the countryside, get some
proper walking shoes and boots first. And make
sure that they fit properly. Wear the shoes at home
several times to see if they press anywhere.
Uncomfortable shoes can be dangerous on a hike.

Pain can lead to danger
A walker can get into trouble if his feet hurt.
Supposing your shoe has rubbed a big blister on
your heel. Every step is agony. You begin to get
irritable with other people. Your judgement is not
quite so good when you are not feeling well. You
can make mistakes in map reading. You could put
your foot down on a loose stone or a tussock of
grass because you cannot bear to walk properly. A
sprain or even a broken ankle could result. Now the
party really is held up — all because of your badly-
fitting footwear!
    Walking shoes should be strongly made and of
leather if possible. The soles must be thick and
ridged so that you cannot feel stones through them.
Two or three miles in a light-soled shoe and you
would be like the princess in the fairy tale — you
could almost feel a pea lying on the ground through
the shoe! Lace-ups are best because they hold the
sides of the foot firmly. A low, square heel is
essential. With your shoes, wear woollen socks.
Take a spare pair with you in your pack. It is a
marvellous feeling to be able to change your socks
before starting the walk back home!

A pair of wheels

Keep your bicycle clean and learn to look after it properly

If you want to cover a lot of miles in a day, cycling is the best way for a young person to travel.

On your bicycle, you can do a one-day exploration trip and get home the same night. Or you can travel further over a weekend and camp overnight. Your bicycle will help you to carry enough camping gear to camp comfortably. When you have done a few weekend trips and you have learned how to look after yourself, you might get together with a group of friends and spend a holiday touring hundreds of miles, camping when and where you feel like it.

And later, when you are older, think of the adventure of touring a whole continent on a bicycle! Thousands of young people do. You can see them, bicycles loaded with packs, cycling through north America, all over Europe, in Australia, South Africa — even in India and the far east! If you would like to know more about international cycling, look at the list of cycling clubs and societies on page 141.

Before you start
Some people do not care if their bicycle is dirty and rusty. As long as it goes along and more or less stops when they brake, that is enough. If you want to use your bike for real travelling, face up to the truth now. If your bike is not properly looked after you are going to have a break-down sooner or later. And you could be miles from a garage, in a deserted place. To be safe and sure on the road, keep your bicycle clean and learn to look after it. There are books about servicing bicycles, specially written for young people. Check these on page 142. Unless you are sure that you know exactly what to do in a break-down emergency, do not start adventuring just yet. Stay near to home.

Bicycle packs

The first thing to remember is that the bicycle should carry the kit and equipment, not the rider. You can try wearing a haversack or a rucksack but after a few miles, you will wish you had not!

There are different kinds of carriers which can be fixed to a bicycle. Bags can be strapped onto the handlebars or fastened behind the saddle. The best kind of carriers for touring and camping holidays are panniers. These hang on special frames fitted to the sides of the bicycle at the rear. For a day's trip, a saddle carrier would be enough to carry what you need. Later, you can get yourself a handlebar carrier.

What to wear

You want to be comfortable when cycling; warm when it is cold and cool when it gets hot. The best cycling outfit is a pair of shorts, a cotton vest or T-shirt, another sleeved shirt on top of that and a windcheater. Your shirt should have big pockets in it if possible — handy for a map, a compass, or something to eat! Stuff a light sweater in your pack if the weather is likely to get colder, as it usually does in the evening. Choose bright colours for everything you wear. It helps motorists to see you. Wear shoes with a firm ridged sole. Sneakers or tennis shoes are not suitable for cycling. They can slip on the pedals and, anyway they feel uncomfortable after a while. Add a lightweight raincape and hat in your pack and you are ready to go. For winter touring, cyclists sometimes wear a light weight track suit instead of shorts and windcheater.

Cyclist's pack

For exploring trips, you do not need to carry very much in your bicycle pack.

Food first

Pack the same kind of food for cycling as you would for a day's hike. If you like sandwiches, choose dry fillings, such as meat or cheese, rather than egg, chopped tomato or sardine. Wet fillings make the bread soggy.

Take apples, biscuits, cookies or cake and something to drink. Water is best. Buy soft drinks on the road if you really want them. Take a hot drink in a vacuum flask if you like hot drinks. Very hot water in a flask and a soup powder in a sachet are easy to carry. Mixed, they make a good satisfying snack for a rest stop. Pack your food in flat, polythene boxes with lids, or in plastic bags. Polythene bottles will strap onto the bicycle frame.

To keep your energy going, (and your spirits up), take some snacks. Carry these where you can get to them easily, such as in your handlebar carrier. Dried fruit — raisins, sultanas, stoned dates — are good and energy-giving. Nuts (not the salted kind), chocolate with fruit and nuts in it, glucose candies or sweets, fruit pastilles or mint cake are delicious and easy to eat.

Essentials

Your bicycle should have a tool kit. Keep it complete and know how to use it. You should also take a small first aid kit and torch. Have enough money with you to make a telephone call or, in a real emergency to buy a train or bus ticket to get you home. Carry money in a buttoned pocket. Take a good map with you, protected in a plastic bag. If it rains, you can check the route without the rain damaging the map. Take a note book and pencil

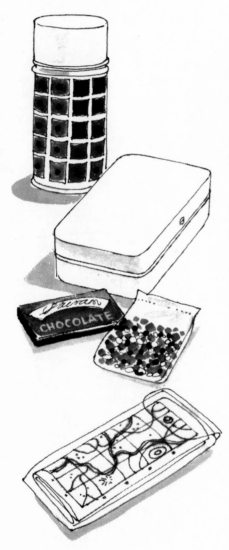

A hot drink in a vacuum flask and some energy-giving snacks

and, if possible, a compass, particularly if you are planning to leave the roads and venture off down tracks and bridlepaths. Write your name and address in your notebook.

Taking precautions

Take a guide book or an information leaflet, if one is available for the area. Knowing a bit about the district makes exploring more rewarding.

Some young people think that letting parents and guardians know where they are going and when they will be back, takes away their freedom. This is the wrong attitude. Leaving information about your movements adds to your freedom. It also prevents people worrying about you unnecessarily. It shows adults that you have a sense of responsibility and know how to behave in an adult fashion. And, if something does go wrong, and you get lost or hurt, people know where to start looking for you.

For instance, supposing a group of hikers were going out on a days trek across wild, mountainous country. They do not tell anyone in which direction they are going, where they hope to end up nor when they expect to be back. A fog comes down or the weather gets very bad. Eventually, someone realises that the hikers have not come back. Search parties are organised. But where do they start? Are the hikers nearly home or have they had an accident on the mountain side? No-one knows anything for sure.

You see how thoughtlessness can cause a lot of trouble. Make sure that your parents know exactly where you are going. Tell them the route you hope to take. Give an approximate time when you can be expected home. And if something happens to delay you, telephone or send a message. It is not only considerate. It makes very good sense.

What kind of map?

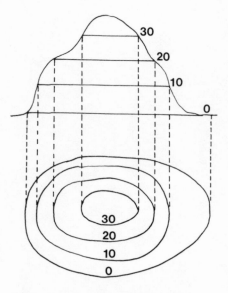

You can work out how high a hill or mountain is from the contour lines

Even though you may think that you know your district very well, it is a good idea to use a map when you are going out on a day's trek or doing some local exploring. For one thing, working from a map is more fun than just drifting off without having a set plan. For another, if you have a map with you and you know how to use it, you are not likely to get lost. You can explore side roads or tracks, knowing where they are going to end up. Perhaps most important of all, a map helps you to plan just how far as you want to go on a journey and get home again at the time you promised.

Everyone should know how to read a map. Many people have to use and understand maps as part of their jobs — surveyors, architects and engineers for example. Soldiers, sailors and airmen learn to use maps as part of their training.

The maps in an atlas are useful for studying the shape of a country, its rivers, mountains and plains etc., but they are not much good for planning a route. You need a map with a lot of detail to do this. Road maps show cities and towns, main roads and highways, secondary and side roads as well as airports and railway tracks. If you were planning to travel only on the roads you could use a road map but it might be a little dull, and anyway, a road map does not tell you much about the countryside itself.

To be able to see exactly what the country is going to be like and to work out a route properly, you need a government Ordnance Survey or topographical map. (They are a bit expensive to buy but worth the money).

These maps are drawn to show the land in a great deal of detail, not just the cities, towns, roads and railway tracks but also the buildings in the towns and in the countryside. Forests and woods are marked with their different kinds of trees.

Lakes, rivers and streams are clearly shown and you can recognise places where the ground might be marshy or stony. These maps also show the mountains and hills and from them you can work out how high a hill is before planning to travel over it. If you were going on a cycling journey for instance, it would be important to know how hilly the roads were going to be so that you could choose the best and easiest route.

Scale and distance
A map is a plan of the land drawn much smaller, and every map is drawn to a scale. The first thing you want to know about your map is the scale, so that you can work out distances between points fairly accurately. Get hold of a map of your district and study it. Somewhere on it you will see the word 'scale' followed by some measurements. Older maps may give the scale as 1 inch to 1 mile but newer maps give metric measurements. Large scale maps, such as ordnance and topographical maps, usually give the scale like this: 1:50,000. This means that 1 centimeter on the map equals 50,000 centimetres (or $\frac{1}{2}$ kilometre) on the ground. A kilometre is about 5/8 mile.

Some maps give the scale as a line marked into segments. This is called a linear scale but the principle is the same. Each of the segments is marked with the number of miles or kilometres it is meant to represent. Once you know what the scale of your map is you can measure the distance between two points and work out just how far you would have to walk or cycle.

Orienting the map

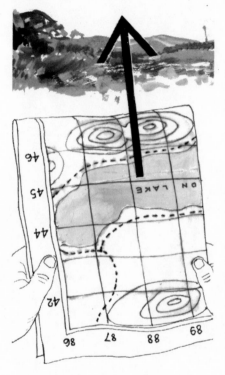

Orienting a map on the route ahead saves you from going the wrong way

When you are looking at a map, always hold it so that the things which are straight ahead of you are also straight ahead on the map. If for instance you are walking towards a hill, hold the map so that the marked hill is in front of you even if the words on the map are upside down. This is called orienting the map and if you always do it you will not run the risk of turning right when you should be turning left which is very easy to do.

Map references

On the edges of a map there are numbers and letters. These are called 'references' and are used to find a place on a map. Look again at the map illustrated. This is an imaginary place. Supposing you are given E4 as a reference. Put your finger on the line marked E and then another finger on the line marked 4. Run the fingers towards each along the lines until they meet. You will see that you have been given the reference for a place called Johnstown. To make sure you understand, find out what the following references are for and try them on a friend.

C3, D5, B1, B4, A1, C2, E2.

Four-figure reference

Look at your large scale ordnance or topographical map again. You will see that it is divided into squares. These are called grid lines. Each of the lines has a number. Because the scale is so large, you cannot use reference numbers to find a place. But you can find the area where the place is. The map has so much detail on it, you can quickly spot the exact place you want. A reference for an area, (a complete square on your map), is called a 'four figure reference'. This is how it works. The line number on the left of the square is given first. Then

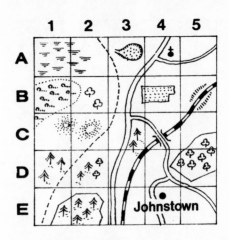

the number for the bottom line of the square is given. On the second map illustrated, an area has been marked. The reference for this would be 8541. If you were doing orienteering, (see page 24), with a club or outdoor organisation, this is the kind of reference you would be given to find a place.

See if you can work out the map references for the quarry, the marsh, a church and an orchard

Pinpointing a spot

But even with a large-scale map, you can still pinpoint a tiny place on the map. This is how it is done. You have the two area numbers. Now you look at the area and, in your mind, you divide it into 10 sections down the left-hand line and ten sections across the bottom line. Look at the illustration. So the first reference is line 85 and section 6. You call it 856. The next reference is line 41 and section 4. It is now called reference 414. Your complete reference for the spot marked x is 856414. And you would know exactly where to find it on the map.

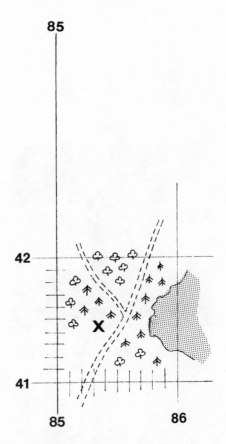

Here is how an area on a map is divided into tenths

In towns, maps show streets and some large buildings to help you to find your way . . .

. . . but in open country, you have to take a sightbearing on hills to follow a route

Sight bearings

A map is like a drawing of the land made from high up in the sky. You can see all the roads and streets in a town. If you wanted to walk from one side of your town to a place on the other, you could easily find the way, using a map. Mark where you are standing with an 'A'. Mark where you are going with a 'B'. The straight line between the two marks is the shortest and best way to travel but you cannot go straight through buildings! So you work out a route on the streets and roads which will take you to B quickly. You might see that if you walked down that main road and took the second road on the right where there is a church, you could go down a long road to a fork. At the fork there is a hospital. You take the left fork and then the second road on the left again. You have got to B. The church and the hospital checked your route for you. You could see that you were on the right track by these two landmarks.

If you were travelling across open country from A to B, you might notice a mountain peak on the horizon ahead of you. As long as that peak was directly ahead of you, you could not go wrong, even though there are no streets or roads. You would just walk towards the peak and, eventually, you would come to B. The hill is your sight bearing.

But if there were no mountains or other land marks that you could use as sight bearings, or if it were dark and a fog was coming up, you could still find your way across country by using a compass.

The compass
There are four main directions, north, south, west and east. Looking at the compass, with north at the top, west is to the left. (You can always remember which way is west and which east because with N to the top, W and E spells 'WE'.) Halfway between

Orienteering

these four main points are north-east, south-east, south-west and north-west.

You could go on and put in more points between these but the words to describe a direction would get very long. To make the compass directions more accurate, the circle of a compass is divided up into 360 points or degrees. Look at the illustration again. East is exactly 90 degrees (90°) on the compass from where north is. When degrees are used to describe a direction, it is called a 'bearing'.

Orienteering

In different parts of the world, an exciting sport called 'orienteering' is played. The players are given a map with several places marked on it and, using a compass, they must discover the bearings and work their way from place to place. The player who gets to all the places in the right order, and then gets to the finishing post first, wins.

You can play a kind of orienteering game with your friends, using an ordinary compass. You must all learn how to work out a bearing before you can play the game. And have a compass each.

Finding a bearing

Get a map of your district. Somewhere near to the top you will see an arrow pointing north. This is the True North. Your compass points to Magnetic North, but we will come back to this later. Mark a cross on the map where you are now. Mark it A. Now mark another cross somewhere on the map, B. Draw a line between A and B. Use your compass to discover which way north lies. Lay the map on the ground so that the north marked on it is lying to the north. Lay your compass on the map so that the pointer lies to north and south. Put the compass on the spot where you are now, marked by the cross.

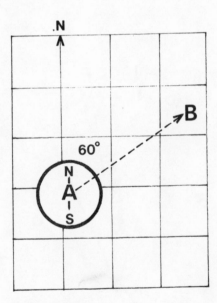

From A to B on a bearing of 60 degrees

Make sure that the grid lines on the map line up with the pointer on your compass.

Now if you look at the degrees round the edge of the compass, you will see that the A — B line you drew matches up with one of the degree bearings. Look at the illustration. The A — B line i on a bearing of 60°. If you were to start walking from the place you have marked with A, with your compass in your hand, walking on a 60° bearing, you would eventually get to the place marked B.

Magnetic North

If you look again at your map, you will see that somewhere near the bottom you are given the number of degrees between True North and Magnetic north in your area. This varies all over th world and changes a little every year. Whatever your map gives as the variation you add, (or substract), to your bearing. If it is *west* of grid north, you add. If it says it is *east* of grid north, you subtract. With the bearing you have just worked out 60°, if the variation were given as '9° W of grid north,' your final bearing would be 69°. 9° may not seem much but at the end of a mile or two, that 9° could put you quite a long wa) from your finishing place!

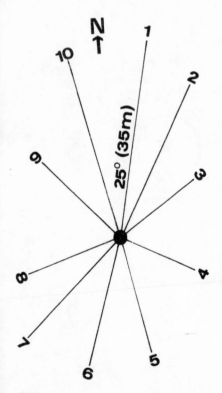

Orienteering game with 10 control points

Orienteering game

Each player has a compass. Before the game starts, the controller player chooses a starting place. From he paces out several control points. They can be as far away from the centre starting place as he likes. Then, at each control point, he puts a small piece of card, face down on the ground, with a code number on it. The controller measures the distance of each control point from start. Then he works out the bearing for each control point from start.

Look at the illustration. This shows you a game set out with a starting point and ten control points. Each player is given a list of the bearings and the distance he must travel along them. Control 1 for instance is 25° and is 35m (38 yds) away.

Each player has to work out the correct bearing, move along it for the correct distance and then check the code card. He writes the code number down on his orienteering card. When he has all the codes, he presents them to the controller for checking. The first person to get all the codes right, wins the game.

Another orienteering game

Having played one orienteering game, try another which is a little harder. This one is best played in a park or an open space. You could even try it over fairly rough country to make it a bit harder! The controller decides on his starting place. He chooses his first bearing and paces it out. He stops when he thinks he has gone far enough and puts a coded marker on the ground, face down. He writes down the bearing and starts off again on a new bearing.

At every check point he puts a coded marker on the ground. He can cross his own path if he chooses. (See illustration.) When he has worked out about 10 bearings and perhaps worked back to the starting place, the game begins.

Each player is given the list of bearings and the distance between them. They go off one by one. Each player has to find the correct bearing and then travel the correct distance. The first player to check all the coded markers and arrive at the finishing place, wins.

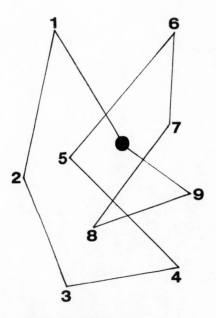

Another orienteering game with a tricky route to follow

Measuring your pace

When you are working out a route on a map, you check the scale and then work out the distances you have to travel. You may see an escape route on your path. (An escape route is a place where you could turn off the path and return home very quickly if the weather suddenly became worse! Treks should have escape routes planned into them after the halfway mark.)

You work out that there is an escape route about 350 metres or yards along the path you are travelling. How will you know when you have walked 350 metres or yards? A man's stride might be about a metre or a yard. A woman's is certainly smaller. A young person's stride might be shorter still. So how do you accurately measure 350 metres or yards?

Here is how it is done
Using a tape measure or a yard stick, accurately mark out 100 metres or yards on the ground. Now walk along it, counting the number of times your right foot touches the ground. Make a note. Now run the distance. Make a note of the number of times your right foot hits the ground. Try it again running and walking uphill, and running and walking downhill.

If you know your pace, you can work out distances. For instance, if you walked 125 paces in the 100 metres or yards, the distance to the escape route will be 525 paces. This will be useful to you in orienteering games. You can accurately pace out the distances between check points.

Pathfinding by the stars

On a clear night when you can see the stars, lie on your back and look at the sky. See if you can recognise some of the star groups. Star gazing or astronomy is a fascinating hobby and great fun if you are sleeping in the open.

If you live in the northern hemisphere (in one of the countries north of the equator) you probably know the groups of stars called the Plough (or the Big Dipper as it is sometimes called). If you can find this group of seven stars, you can easily find the North star and this will always tell you the direction of the true north. The North star never sets and so it is always in the same place in the sky. The position of the Plough changes with the seasons as the earth moves along its orbit.

Finding the North star
Look at the illustration; the Plough has four stars making the base of the plough shape and three more making the curved handle. The two stars at the front end of the plough shape are called the Pointers. To find the North star, take your eye along the two Pointers and across the empty space. The next star in line is the North star.

The Plough looks upside down in winter. Make sure you know how it looks in both summer and winter or you may confuse it with another group called Pegasus.

The Southern Cross
If you live in the southern hemisphere, in South Africa, Australia or New Zealand, you can see stars and star groups that people in the northern hemisphere never see. The most brilliant star in the southern sky is a yellow star called Canopus. This is in a group called the Ship.

Canopus is the most brilliant star in the whole

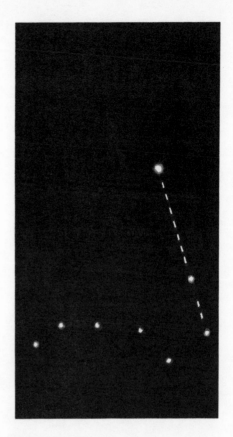

The North star in the northern hemisphere sky always points the direction of true north

The Southern Cross in the southern hemisphere sky shows the direction of true south

of the sky. Astronomers say that it shines as brightly as 80,000 suns put together!

The most easily recognised star group in the southern sky is the Southern Cross. This has four bright stars close together. Like the North star, the Southern Cross never changes its position and shows the direction of true south.

Star gazing

Star gazing can also help you to find your way at night. Supposing it is a cloudy night and you can only see one or two stars. Here is a way of checking your direction. Find a long straight stick and somewhere to rest your elbows — a wall will do. Hold one end of the stick against your shoulder as if it were a rifle. Look along the stick and aim it at a star. Try and keep the stick absolutely still. After about a minute, the star will appear to move a little. This is because the earth is spinning round. You will have to watch for the movement very carefully because it is slight.

In the northern hemisphere: if the star moves to the left of your aimed stick, you are facing the north. If it moves to the right, you are facing south. If the star appears to move upwards, you are facing east and if it seems to move downwards, you are facing west.

In the southern hemisphere: a move left means you are facing south. A move to the right, you are facing north. Up, you are facing west, down, facing east. Try this yourself, using a compass. It is an interesting experiment.

Which way, what time?

Compass from a wrist watch

Although you need a proper compass for orienteering and for working out bearings, you can use your wrist watch for finding out which way north lies. It can only be done in the daytime, when the sun is shining and not at exactly midday when the sun is overhead.

How it is done

Supposing it is 8 o'clock in the morning. Lay the watch on a flat surface, the 8 towards the sun. The direction which is exactly halfway between the 8 and the 12 on the watch face, (where the 10 is on this occasion), points south (if you are in the northern hemisphere), so you know that the opposite direction is north. If you are in the southern hemisphere, the halfway mark between the hour and the 12 points north and of course, the opposite direction is south. Try this yourself, using a compass to check your findings.

Compass from a needle

Here is another way to make a 'compass' which will show north and south. You need a magnet and a needle. Hold the needle in one hand and the magnet in the other. With only one leg of the magnet, brush along the length of the needle about 20 times. At the end of each stroke, take the magnet into the air and round in a half circle before starting the next stroke.

Tie a piece of thread to the middle of the needle so that it hangs. When the needle stops swinging it will point north and south. Try magnetizing a needle in this way and then hold it over your compass. Watch what happens!

A watch or a clock can be used to work out the north and south

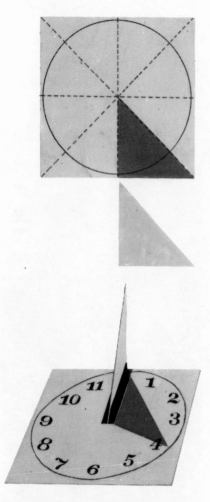

Here is how to draw the lines on the sun-dial's face. The shaded section is the shape and size of the sun-dial's arm

Simple sun-dial

Long before clocks were made, people told the time of day by the position of the sun in the sky. A sun-dial works on this principle. You can make a simple sun-dial which will tell you Greenwich Mean Time on a sunny day.

How to do it

Cut the back from a cardboard cereal packet. Lay a saucer or a small plate on the card and draw round it to make a circle. With a ruler, draw lines from top to bottom and from side to side. Draw another line diagonally from corner to corner. And then another line diagonally from corner to corner. Look at the illustration. Next, shade one section. Cut a piece of card to exactly this shape and size. Trace it off if this is the easiest way. This piece is the arm of the sun-dial which throws the shadow.

Mark the circle with numbers like a clock face — you already have the marks for 3, 6, 9 and 12. Now you must fix the arm to the face of the sun-dial. Stand the arm along the line between the middle of the dial and the 12. It fits exactly. Tape the arm along both sides with sticky tape to make it stand up. Now the sun-dial is ready to use. Lay it on the ground with the 6 pointing towards north (or south in the southern hemisphere). The sun will throw the shadow of the arm down onto the dial and the number the shadow points to is the time of day (Greenwich Mean Time). If you live in Britain, where the clock is put forward one hour in the spring (Summer Time) you must make allowances for this and add one hour.

When weather gets bad

In the northern hemisphere particularly, the weather
on hills and mountains changes very suddenly. You
can be just an hour or two out and suddenly, down
comes the mist or it begins to snow. Do you go on
or turn back? This is a decision that even people
who are used to trekking find difficult to make. A
young person without experience finds it very hard
to decide. You are warm and not in the least tired.
You have made up your mind that you are going to
get 'there', and the change in weather adds to the
excitement. 'Now, this is a real adventure,' you say
to yourself.

Think again
This is a time when your sense of responsibility
must be stronger than anything else you are feeling.
Play it safe. There is no shame in turning back. If
you have planned an 'escape route' into your trek
this is the time to use it if you can.
But be sensible — not daring and 'brave'. An
experienced adventurer knows when to take risks
and has worked out the chances of success. When
you have been properly trained to work out the
risks involved and do the right thing in an
emergency, as an adventure school would teach you,
only then you can start taking chances.

If you were nearly home of course, you would
have to cope with the weather anyway and go on.
In fog and thick mist, you would do what a pilot
has to do, 'fly blind', using your compass and map.
If you have done your 'homework' and your
bearings are properly worked out, your navigation
should be good enough to get you home safely.

Learning about weather

Holly berries do not necessarily mean a hard winter — but some country sayings are true

How often have you heard someone make a prediction about weather like 'The snails are burrowing deep — that means a hard winter!' Or, 'A lot of berries on the holly bush — that means early frost and snow.'

Are these, and other, sayings true predictions? Some of them are the results of country people's observations. Over generations, they have watched the changes in nature and the behaviour of animals and birds. These sayings from country lore are often based on scientific fact and can be relied upon. In the short term, however, some sayings can be misleading. 'Red sky at night, shepherd's delight', for instance. A red sky is not necessarily a sign of good weather. If you were planning to go for a day's walk across difficult country you would be very unwise if you relied upon this kind of prediction!

The only safe way to check on the weather before venturing on a long trek is by contacting your local meterological station. They can give you information about the weather for up to 12 hours ahead. They can also make a fairly accurate prediction about what is likely to happen to the weather in the next 20 hours.

Radio and television stations also give local weather forecasts. Some newspapers print weather maps which you can look at for a general picture.

It helps you to make decisions about your route and the distance you can travel if you understand the information weathermen and forecasters give you. You can also learn how to forecast weather changes yourself by reading the sky and observing the direction from which the wind is blowing.

Understanding weather

Before you can begin to understand what makes the weather change, you have to know about the air around us. Weather is changed by the wind. Wind is moving air. So what makes the air move?

The earth's atmosphere
The earth has a layer of air round it called the 'atmosphere'. The atmosphere is about 200 miles deep. It is a mixture of different gases. Near to the earth's surface, the air has enough of the gases in it to make it possible for us to breathe and for life to flourish. Further out in space, at about 60 miles up, there is no breathable air at all. The air is 'thinner'.

The 'thicker' air, with its mixture of gases, near to the earth's surface 'pushes' against everything on earth from every side. This push is called 'air pressure'. Scientists have worked out that normal air pressure on earth is 15lbs on every square inch of everything — including you and me. You might think that this is a very great weight for people to carry around but our bodies are used to it and we do not notice.

Experiment showing air pressure
Do this easy experiment to show yourself that air pressure exists. Fill a small glass with water. Lay a piece of thick paper on top of the glass. Put one hand on the card and pick up the glass. Turn the glass upside down and then take your hand away. The paper will stay in place and keep the water in. It looks like magic! It is the air pressure keeping the paper in place. The air pressure pushing up from under the glass is 15lbs on every square inch of the paper's surface. The air pressure pushing down is still 15lbs but there are not so many square inches of paper showing. Some is covered up by the glass of water. So the pressure pushing up is stronger

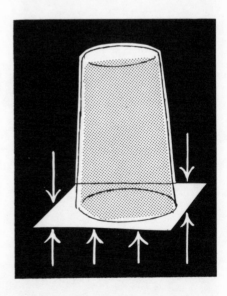

An interesting experiment with water and air pressure

and holds the paper in place. The weight of the water makes no difference.

Changes in air pressure

When the air around us is heated up by the sun, it expands. Molecules, the word used to describe minute groups of atoms which make up the gases in the air, get further apart and spread out. The air has become 'thinner'.

The countries near to the equator get the sun's rays shining directly down on them almost all day. The countries in the northern hemisphere get the sun's rays at an angle and the heat of the sun is less. Look at the diagram and you will understand.

The sun is therefore heating up some parts of the earth's surface more than others. The air over these places gets heated too, expands and gets thinner. As air becomes thinner, the pressure gets less. It becomes 'low pressure'.

Countries near to the earth's equator get the full heat of the sun's rays

The air pressure round the world must even itself up, so the higher pressure air, over the cold lands and seas, moves to fill the low pressure places. If the difference between the temperature of the hot places and the cold places is a lot, then the air moves faster. We feel the moving air as wind.

You have probably felt the effect of this yourself. If you have been on a beach on a very hot day in summer you may have felt a breeze blowing from the cooler sea towards the hotter land. At night, when the sun has gone, the land cools down quicker than the sea. The cool breeze blows from the land towards the warmer sea.

So now you know what makes the wind. Wind brings changes in the weather with it, depending on which direction the wind is coming from. Weathermen get information about air pressure from weather stations in different parts of the world.

From this, they know what is going to happen to the winds. But how do meteorologists tell what the air pressure is?

Cool air from above the sea moves towards the hotter land as a breeze

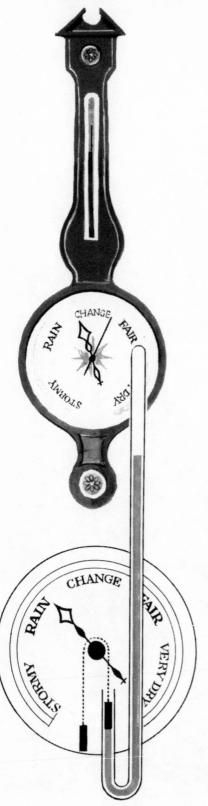

The barometer

The pressure of the air is always changing. Sometimes the air is 'thick' or dense, sometimes it is 'thinner' and less dense. The density of the air makes the pressure. Pressure is measured by an instrument called a barometer.

You have probably seen barometers. They usually hang in a hallway. They have a round dial with a pointer on it and a long case above the dial. There are words round the dial, 'stormy, rain, change, fair, set fair and dry'. The words do not in fact mean very much. They are simply an indication that the pressure is changing and the barometer's mechanism is moving the hands on the dial.

Weathermen use a more complicated kind of barometer which shows the air pressure in inches, but the working principle of both kinds of barometer is similar.

Look at the illustration of the barometer's works. This is how the barometer registers changes in pressure. The pointer on the dial is moved by weights. In the barometer case there is a long tube containing mercury. At the top of the tube is a space with no air in it. So there is no air pressure here. At the other end of the tube is the surface of the mercury with a weight floating on it. As the air pressure gets higher and 'pushes' down, the mercury is forced along the tube to fill the space at the other end. The floating weight goes down with the level of the mercury. This pulls the pointer round the dial to 'fair'.

The air pressure drops, the mercury rises in the tube and the floating weight goes up. The second weight pulls the pointer round to 'rain'.

When the pressure drops, we know that high pressure cold air is going to rush in to balance the air pressure. The winds that come will bring a change in the weather.

Depressions — what are they?

Sometimes you will hear a weatherman say something like 'the depression centred over such and such a place is moving in a north-easterly direction'. On hearing this, you might wonder whether this means that the weather where you are is going to get better.

The word 'depression' is used to describe a low pressure area. Weathermen know that when a depression has happened, they can expect winds from a high pressure area. They also know something else. Winds do not blow in a straight line. Winds blow in a spiral round a depression. They go round in an anti-clockwise direction — the opposite way to the clock's hands. Look at the illustration. So, if you stand with your back to the wind, the depression area is always on your left. You can check on which way the depression is moving.

Winds bring weather changes

The movement of air and the spin of the world on its axis makes some winds blow in the same direction all the time. These winds were used by old-time sailing ships so that merchants could carry goods about the world. South of the equator, between the great land masses, winds blow from the south pole towards the tropics. These are called the south-east trade winds. Between the big land masses of North and South America and Africa and Europe, there are two trade winds. One is called the 'south westerlies' and would have taken ships from the Americas to Europe. The other is called the 'north-east trade wind' and carried ships from Spain to Africa and South America. You can see how useful they must have been to the traders.

Winds bring weather changes

The winds from the north and east are cold while west winds bring rain

The winds blowing from the south-west across Britain and northern Europe have come from warm, southern countries. But, because they have blown across the Atlantic Ocean too, they are wet winds and may bring rain. The west wind, coming across the sea, brings rain as well. In the northern hemisphere, the wind coming from the north comes from the arctic and is cold. The wind from the east has come across the mass of Europe from Siberia and is usually cold and dry. So you can see how winds can bring a change in the weather depending on the direction they are coming from.

What makes it rain — or snow?

The heat of the sun draws up water from the surface of the earth, from the seas, the lakes and rivers. The sun turns the water into vapour and this rises up into the atmosphere. Water vapour is invisible but when it gets up into the cooler air, it turns back into tiny droplets of water. We see these floating drops of water as clouds. As more and more drops of water form, they join together to make bigger drops. Then they fall to earth as rain.

If the upper atmosphere is very cold, the vapour cools down, not just into water, but turns into ice. The tiny specks of ice join together and make snow-flakes.

Reading the clouds

When there are big black clouds overhead, anyone can tell that it is going to rain. Clouds can tell you other things about the weather too. There are three main types of clouds. They have Latin names, Cirrus, Cumulus and Stratus.

Cirrus The Latin word cirrus means 'curl'. It is used to describe what this cloud looks like. Cirrus clouds

Reading the clouds

are very high. They look wispy and white against a blue sky. Winds, very high in the atmosphere, are breaking clouds up into wisps. This means that the weather will change fairly soon.

Stratus The Latin word stratus means 'layers' and this describes the cloud. Stratus is a solid layer of cloud, sometimes hanging quite low over the earth. The layers can be very thick, as much as 2000 ft above the earth's surface. Stratus clouds sometimes form over the sea coast in summer. Usually, if they form early in the day, the sun 'dries up' the clouds and the weather is sunny later. When a low pressure area is moving across hill country, there can be low clouds and fog at the same time. Stratus over hill country usually means that it could rain for several days.

When the cloud layers start to break up again and the wind begins to drop, the cloud formation is called **Strato-cumulus.** It might still rain a bit but good weather is on the way.

Cumulus The Latin word means 'gathering or accumulating'. Cumulus clouds are white and look like cauliflowers with flat bases. They always appear in good weather but if they start to form themselves early in the day, it could rain later. When cumulus clouds begin to get tall and tower into the sky, looking as though they were boiling up, they sometimes take on a shape like a blacksmith's anvil. This cloud formation is called **cumulo-nimbus,** (the word 'nimbus' means rain). This means a heavy downpour of rain is on the way, perhaps even a storm by the evening.

There is another type of cumulus which forms very high in the sky. These clouds look a little like the scales of a fish and the effect is sometimes called a 'mackerel sky'. This means very changeable weather.

On the next pages, you can see how clouds can help you to tell what is happening to the weather

Cumulus *clouds mean warm, fine weather but if they are in the sky very early in the morning, there might be a shower of rain later*

Stratus *clouds is usually low over the land and makes the air feel cooler. It always means rain in the northern hemisphere but sometimes, in summer, the heat of the sun can dry up the banks of clouds and the day turns fine later*

Stratus-cumulus *clouds mean the weather is breaking up and could get better*

Cirrus *looks like thin whispy clouds very high up and means that there are very strong winds at high altitude. The weather is about to change*

Cirro-cumulus *is sometimes called a 'mackerel' sky. In summer, it means the weather is getting better but in winter, it can mean frost at night, or fog coming*

Cumulo-nimbus *clouds are a sign of rain, sometimes of a storm. The shape of the cumulo-nimbus cloud is a bit like a blacksmith's anvil*

First aid kit

Exploration expeditions nearly always have a doctor on the team. He usually has to be an expert in the kinds of illnesses and accidents which can happen. An expedition into the arctic or up a mountain would need a doctor who knew about treating frostbite or snow blindness. A jungle trek would need someone who was an expert on fevers and snake bites.

It helps an adventurer to know something about the kinds of accidents and illnesses which can happen on an expedition. One day, you might be on a hike or out camping and a friend gets sunstroke or is bitten by an insect. It is useful to be able to help and do the right thing.

First aid
Certain kinds of accidents can happen when people are living outdoors or travelling. It is a good idea to make yourself the 'expedition doctor' by having a first aid kit in your pack. You do not need very much equipment, (unless of course you are going to be camping for several weeks).

Fitting out a first aid kit
First aid kits can be bought but you can make a very good one yourself. Find a tin box with a lid, roughly 200mm x 125mm (8in x 5in). Clean it properly with soap and hot water inside and out. Dry it with a clean cloth.
Put inside the tin:
Packet of plaster dressings in assorted sizes
2 small and 1 medium-sized sterilized dressings
(Sterilized dressings are a gauze pad on a long bandage. They have been treated to kill any germs that might be on them and are sealed in a paper packet. Do not open the packet until you are ready to use the dressing.)

Packet of lint
Small pair of scissors
Long strip of 50mm (3in)-wide stretchy plaster
    dressing
Small tube of antiseptic cream
Pair of tweezers, safety pins
Small plastic bottle of vinegar
Small packet of bicarbonate of soda

Using your first aid kit
Never try to treat anything serious. You can help
with small cuts and grazes, by cleaning them up and
putting on a plaster. Stings and bites hurt quite a
lot and it helps to stop the pain a little. Burns and
scalds can be helped if they are just reddening of the
skin. But for serious cuts and bad stings, burns and
scalds, always get the person who has been hurt to a
doctor just as quickly as you can.

Here are just a few simple treatments which are
useful to know about if you are trekking or
camping.

Blisters on the feet If you have to go on
walking, cover the blister with a strip of stretchy
plaster dressing. Put your sock on. Do not break
blisters open. When you can rest, put a dry
sterilized dressing over the blister and let it dry up.

Cuts and grazes Let the wound bleed a bit. It
helps to clean it. Wash all round the wound with
soap and water — not over it — using a piece of
lint. Put a plaster dressing over the wound if it is
small, or a sterilized dressing if it is bigger. If the
wound goes on hurting and the skin round it gets
red, go to the doctor as soon as you can.

Burns and scalds Accidents happen so easily in
camp. People lift hot pots from the fire with bare
hands, or a cooking pot which is not properly
balanced on the fire falls over. Always have a

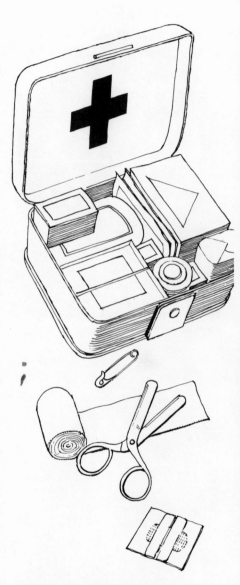

*A first aid box is an important
piece of equipment in a camping pack*

Stings and bites

Vinegar to treat wasp stings and bicarbonate of soda on bee stings. Try and remember which goes on which so you know what to do

bucket of cold water near to a fire because the best thing to do when you get a burn or a scald is to plunge the hurt part into cold water immediately. This takes the heat out of the burn. If a blister comes up do not break it, just go to the doctor as quickly as possible. Otherwise, cover the burn or scalded place with a sterilized dressing.

Stings and bites

All over the world, campers are pestered by insects which sting or bite — and sometimes by snakes too. People do not get bitten by snakes all that often. If you live in a country where there are snakes, you probably already know that you should always wear strong boots and thick socks when out on a trek or a camping trip.

Not all snakes have poisonous bites. A poisonous snake leaves two or three fang marks in the skin. A non-poisonous snake leaves a ring of small teeth marks. If you should get bitten by a snake, try and get a good look at it so that you can describe it to the doctor. He will then know how to treat your bite.

Spiders and scorpions

In tropical and sub-tropical countries, bites from scorpions and spiders can be really serious. Get the victim to a doctor just as quickly as possible.

Stings

Bees sting only once and leave their sting in you. Lift the sting out with tweezers. Mix a little bicarbonate of soda powder with hot water and dab it on the stung place with a piece of lint. (Bicarbonate of soda will not dissolve in cold water. If no hot water is on hand, mix the powder to a thick paste with cold water and dab this on).

Wasps and hornets can sting more than once. The worst place to be stung by a wasp is in the mouth. It is so easy not to notice a wasp sitting on the apple you are eating! Dab wasp stings with vinegar. Hornet stings are more serious. Dab with vinegar and get the victim to a doctor quickly.

Note: so that you remember what to put on wasp or bee stings, try to remember it like this. B goes on bee stings (bicarbonate of soda). V is before W in the alphabet and vinegar goes on wasp (and hornet) stings.

Insect bites

In some parts of the world, mosquitoes are a real pest to campers. It is the female mosquito that makes the whining noise and bites you so painfully. Chemists and drugstores sell Oil of Citronella. It has a strong smell and usually keeps insects away if you use a lot of it on the parts of your skin which are not covered with clothing. Once bitten, there is not much you can do except to dab the bitten place with bicarbonate of soda. Treat gnat, midge and black-fly bites in the same way.

Animal bites

If you camp in the wilds, you might be bitten by an animal which has rabies. Rabies is a terrible disease and although people often associate it only with dogs, all kinds of other animals can have it. Wolves, foxes, bears and skunks, rats, jackals and hyenas can all carry rabies. If a human gets bitten by a rabies-carrying animal, he will die unless he gets to a doctor and has treatment quickly. There is no way of telling if a wild animal is carrying rabies so treat all wild animal bites as serious and get help quickly.

Many wild animals can carry rabies so if you get bitten in camp, you must go to a doctor quickly

Sunburn and sunstroke

Generally, children have far more sense than adults about sunburn. They are not so keen on spending time lying about in the sun getting a tan and so sunburn may be something you have never had to worry about.

On a hike, sunburn can be a real danger because the sun's rays can burn even through hazy cloud. And if you are near to a lake or on a beach, the sun is much stronger if it is shining onto water or sand (and snow too incidentally). The surface of the water or snow acts like a mirror. The sun reflects itself and the heat of it is doubled!

If you do not want to spoil the whole adventure for everyone by complaining about burnt arms or legs, take some care and remember the dangers.

Obviously, if you have been spending a lot of time outdoors, you will have got brown already. But light-skinned people and those with red hair hardly ever go brown and are almost certain to burn. Even coloured people can get sunburn if they have been living in a cold country for a while!

Avoiding sunburn
Rub a sun-filtering cream into your skin if you are likely to burn. Wear long-sleeved tops and trousers to cover up your arms and legs. If you are walking in the noon-day sun, wear a brimmed hat to protect your nose and lips and the back of your neck. Never fall asleep lying in the sun!

Treating sunburn
Dip some lint or cotton wool in cold water and wrap it over the burn. This helps to lessen the pain. Smear a little antiseptic cream over the burn before you go to bed.

Sunstroke

In countries where the sun is very hot, people
sometimes get heatstroke or sunstroke if they have
to work or walk in the blazing sun for a long time.
The body gets too hot. The parts of the body that
help it to lose heat stop working. You can tell
when someone is suffering from sunstroke because
they will say that they feel very thirsty, sick and
dizzy. The skin feels hot and dry and they have a
temperature. There is not enough water in the body
to make any sweat! To help, get the sick person into
the shade or inside where it is cool. Make them lie
down and put cold, wet cloths on the face, round
the neck and under the arms to help the body to
cool down. Dip shirts in water and wring them out
or use towels if they are handy. Sunstroke is very
serious and you should send for a doctor
immediately.

Protect your eyes

If you are trekking and the sun is shining off sand,
water or snow, you are soon going to have sore
eyes. The sun reflects strongly off these mirror-like
surfaces. Perhaps you wear sunglasses in strong
sunlight anyway but try making yourself an eye
protector so that you know what to do in a real
emergency. You can make an eye shield from a
piece of cardboard with eye slits cut in it, tying the
shield round your head. Easier still, tie a piece of
string round your forehead and tuck leaves or ferns
under the string so that they fall over your eyes.
You will be able to see quite clearly but the glare
will be cut down.

*If the sun is bright and hurts your
eyes, make an eyeshield with cardboard
or with grasses or ferns*

Exposure

Even in summer, it can be quite cold when the sun
goes down and you need an extra sweater to put on
in the evening. When you are on a day's walk across
easy country or camping out on a holiday you will
not have much trouble with real cold, but it is an
important part of survival to know the dangers that
can exist in bad weather.

You have probably read about climbers who
have been caught by bad weather and sometimes
one of them suffers from something called
'exposure'. Exposure is another word for
'hypothermia'.

Hypothermia is the word that doctors use. It
means that the person is slowly dying through being
too cold right inside them. Old people can die of
hypothermia on an ordinary cold day in a
temperate climate. It is not extreme cold which
causes it but several things together. For instance, if
a climber is not quite fit and gets tired and
exhausted, and suddenly the air gets colder and the
wind and rain come up, these are the conditions
under which hypothermia can occur. Hypothermia
can be recognised when someone you know begins
to behave in a different way. They behave as though
they might be drunk, perhaps staggering, or their
speech becomes odd and blurred. Sometimes, people
lose interest in what they are doing or go very quiet.
They may get angry and complain about everything.
They will probably shiver without being able to stop
it. Hypothermia is most likely to attack people who
have been a bit foolish about wearing the proper
clothes on a trek in winter. But it can attack
someone who is properly dressed but is trapped
outdoors in bad weather conditions overnight. This
has sometimes happened to climbing teams. If you
should ever be with someone who seems to have
hypothermia, here is what you can do.

Frostbite

Emergency action for exposure

If you are near shelter, try and get there. If not, get
the victim out of the wind and cold. If you have a
tent, put it up. If not, get behind rocks or trees or
build a wall with anything — packs, stones, even
lumps of snow. Whatever you do, you must keep
the victim warm and stop any more heat from
trickling out of his body. Pile everyone's clothes on
him. Make sure he is sitting on something too. If
you have a sleeping bag, put the victim into it.
Someone else should get in too and hug him.
Otherwise, all of you in the party should hug him,
while two go for help. Give him warm drinks if
possible. Do not get him near to a fire. When help
comes, the doctor will make sure that the victim is
warmed slowly. If you can remember what to do,
you will have helped a lot and may save a life.

Frostbite

Frostbite is something that walkers and climbers
have to be careful about in extreme winter. In
normal conditions, such as a day's walking, you
might have very cold hands and feet and your nose
may feel as though it has dropped off, but you
would not be likely to get frostbite. Especially if you
have been wise about clothes and you are wearing
stout boots, warm gloves and a hat. Frostbite
happens when people have been walking in the
freezing air for a very long time. They become tired,
move more slowly and their bodies gradually
become colder and colder. The blood moves more
slowly through the body. The pink look of the skin
fades and it becomes stiff, waxy and yellowish. The
tips of the fingers and the toes are not getting a
proper flow of blood and so the flesh itself begins to
harden.

When you feel cold on a winter's day you jump

up and down, banging your hands and arms on your own body. This is exactly the right thing to do. You are keeping your blood moving round your body. But it is a good idea to know what to do if you think someone is getting frostbitten.

Mountaineers and arctic explorers watch each other's faces for signs of frostbite. Dead-looking white spots appear on the skin. The first thing to do is to get the victim out of the cold air and into a shelter. The frostbitten parts must be warmed against bare skin, preferably someone else's. If you are on your own and your hands seem to be frostbitten, put your hands between your bare thighs or under your arms. If there are two of you, sit facing each other. Each warms the other's feet in his lap. This is what Dougal Haston and Doug Scott, the two men who climbed Mount Everest in 1975, did. They had to spend a night 350 ft below the summit in a tiny bivouac. To stop their feet from freezing they took off their boots and each warmed the other's feet.

Frostbitten skin should never be rubbed hard, and especially not rubbed with snow. The skin could easily be broken and the condition would be much worse. Keep frostbite victims away from the fire. Gradual warming up is the best and safest way.

Signalling for help

When walkers or climbers are missing and search parties go out to look for them, sometimes aircraft are used. If you should ever be stranded somewhere where you can only be found from the air, you have to make sure that you can be seen. It is very difficult for a pilot to see a figure on the ground, even if he is looking for it. Here is what to do.

Three bonfires, 100 paces apart in a triangle, is a ground-to-air signal all pilots recognise

Build a fire

If an aircraft were looking for you, it would be flying low. The pilot would see a smoke signal easily. Light a fire and keep it going with wood and some green leaves, to make a lot of smoke. Better still, build three bonfires, each 100 paces apart and in a triangle. This is a distress signal that is recognised by pilots all over the world.

Other kinds of signals

What do you do if you have nothing to light a fire with? You can make a ground signal which can be seen from the air. If there are stones and shrubs, drag them together and heap them up. Make a big S.O.S. on the ground in the open. Heap the stuff as high as you can so that a shadow is thrown in the sunlight. This makes the signal easier to see. You would have to make the letters really big, about 6m (20ft) tall. Pace this out the next time you are in an open space to see how big the signal letters would have to be.

What other kinds of signals would a pilot see?

If you were on snow, you could shuffle your feet along in the snow to make tracks in the shapes of letters. Shuffled footprint letters would work in sand too but it would be even better if you dug down into the sand along the lines as well so that the heaped sand threw a shadow in the sunlight.

Using a mirror flash

You can use the Morse code to signal for help on
land or on sea by flashing with a mirror or the
shiny lid of a tin can. Flash signals are easy to see
on a sunny day and would quickly attract the
attention of rescuers. Practise flashing with the help
of a friend. Work out some simple signals so that
you know immediately by his reply whether or not
you have been flashing properly. You can stand
quite a distance apart from each other.

How to flash with a mirror
Hold the mirror in your hand. Hold the other hand
out in front of your face. Stand facing in the
direction where you want the flash to be seen. Hold
the mirror in one hand, your fingers on the rim.
Stretch your other arm out in front of you with the
palm of your hand towards your face. Tilt the
mirror until you see the reflection of the sun on
your outstretched hand. Now, if you lower your
arm but keep the hand holding the mirror where it
is, your friend will see the flash. Quick flicks of the
mirror pick up the sun's reflection and make
repeated flashes. With a little practise, you will be
able to time your flashes so that you can signal in
the Morse code.

Signalling with a flashlight
A flashlight or torch will be seen for quite a
distance at night. If you are signalling in an
emergency, such as for rescue, you would find it
easier to signal dots and dashes by putting your
hand over the front of the flashlight rather than
switching on and off.

Whistle signals
An International Mountain Distress signal has been
agreed all over the world so that mountaineers and

climbers can signal to each other for help. The
signal is six long blasts on a whistle, followed by a
minute's pause and then another six long blasts. If
the signal is heard, it is replied to with three long
blasts, a wait, then three more blasts. No matter
what he is doing, a mountaineer always responds to
the signal if he hears it. Always remember this
distress signal but never use it for fun. It would be a
very stupid thing to do and might prevent a rescue
team from going to someone who really did need
help.

Morse Code

A	· —	N	— ·
B	— · · ·	O	— — —
C	— · — ·	P	· — — ·
D	— · ·	Q	— — · —
E	·	R	· — ·
F	· · — ·	S	· · ·
G	— — ·	T	—
H	· · · ·	U	· · —
I	· ·	V	· · · —
J	· — — —	W	· — —
K	— · —	X	— · · —
L	· — · ·	Y	— · — —
M	— —	Z	— — · ·

Signalling with flags

Semaphore was a way of signalling invented by the French. It worked with a system of the Napoleonic wars, in the early 19th century, the British adapted the system. Semaphore machines were built along the coast and across the country so that warnings of an invasion could be sent to London during the day. At night, beacon bonfires were lit.

The British machine had movable arms, rather like a railway signal. Later, men were used to send semaphore messages, using two flags.

Semaphore is a useful way of signalling across open country during the day. Two friends can memorise the code (or copy it out and take it with you) and then stand a long way apart and send messages.

When you are practising semaphore, it helps your partner to recognise your signals if the flags are in different colours. Make one red and the other yellow. Later, you should be able to read signals sent with pieces of white cloth held in each hand.

The semaphore code is on the next page. The figure is drawn from the back and this makes sure that when you are learning the signs, you do them just as the illustration shows. The best way to learn semaphore is to work through the signs from A to Z, moving your arms as though they were the hands of a clock. Say the alphabet aloud to yourself.

Start with one flag in your left hand and down in front of your legs at the 6 o'clock position. Hold the other flag in your right hand at the 7 o'clock position. This is the signal for 'A'.

Look at the code. You will see that to make 'B' you move your right arm up a bit to the 9 o'clock position. For 'C' it goes a bit higher still to the 11 o'clock position. The first 7 letters of the alphabet, A to G, are signalled moving the right hand only. The left hand stays at the 6 o'clock position.

THE SEMAPHORE ALPHABET

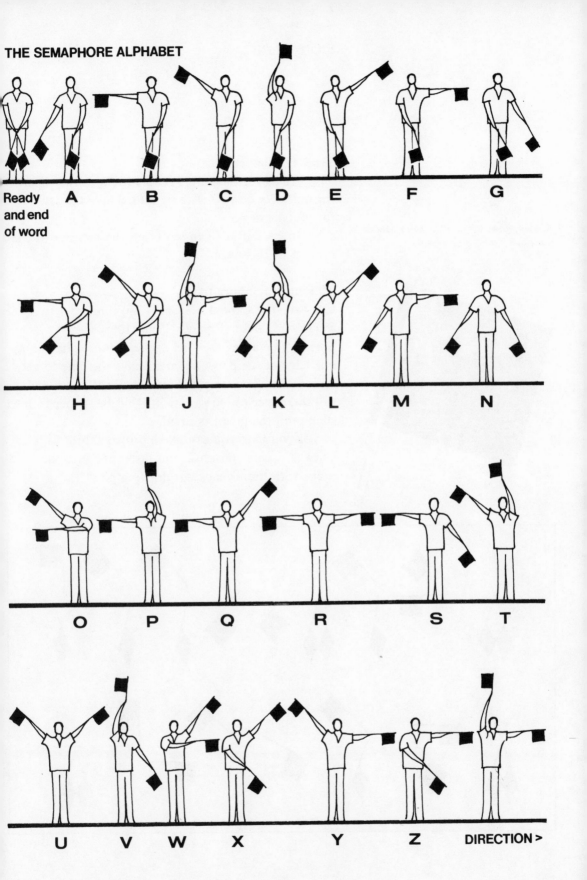

Ready
and end
of word

A   B   C   D   E   F   G

H   I   J   K   L   M   N

O   P   Q   R   S   T

U   V   W   X   Y   Z   DIRECTION >

55

Sending numbers

The signals for the letters A to J are also the signals for numbers 1 to 10. The signal for K is the same for nought to zero.

Now see if you can work out the message at the bottom of this page.

Making semaphore flags

Cut two sticks about 37.5cm (15in) long. Cut two squares of coloured paper 25cm (10in) square. Spread glue along the stick. Spread more glue along one edge of the paper square. Leave the glue to get a bit tacky. Place the stick on the glued paper and roll the paper round the stick. Hold the paper to the stick until the glue has dried.

If you like, you can make proper fabric flags. Cut the squares of fabric and fasten them to the sticks with thumb tacks or drawing pins.

A semaphore flag to make from paper, a stick and some glue

Indian signs

American Indian scouts used all kinds of woodcraft
signs to leave a trail which could be followed. The
signs were small and, because they were made of
natural things — grass blades, small stones, sticks of
wood and so on — the signs were often missed by
people who were not looking for them.

Hunters use similar signs. So do vagrants and
wanderers. You might have noticed a chalked mark
on a gatepost and wondered who could have put it
there and what it meant. This might be a sign left
by a vagrant who had had a good meal given to
him at the house. He is letting other vagrants know
that the house owner is sympathetic!

Work out some Indian signs for yourself and
see if you and your friends can follow the route
marked out. Indian signs are quite useful if there
are only two of you in a camp. One might have
gone to look for wood and the other for water. It
helps if you can each let the other know what you
are doing if there is no way to leave a written note.

Woodsmen use signs too. If a woodsman gets
lost in a big forest and fears that he may be walking
round and round in circles, he cuts 'blazes' into the
bark of trees. A 'blaze' is a small slice of bark cut
from a tree. If he should see a 'blaze' that he has
made, knows that he has been that way before and
makes another attempt to get his bearings. 'Blazes'
can also show a search party which way a lost
person has gone.

It is usually against the law for anyone to cut
'blazes' into trees on private and public land so do
not try it as an Indian sign. It is much better to
bend twigs or leave stone and wood signs which do
no damage.

SIGNALLING

Here are some ideas for signs

Not this way Two sticks on the path, laid in a cross.

This is the way You could use three sticks laid in an arrow head for an obvious sign. For a less obvious sign, tie a knot in a clump of grass on the side of the path or stand a small stone on top of a larger stone.

Take the right (or left) fork Break a small branch on a bush so that the tip points to the right or left. Or put a small stone beside a larger stone. Indians sometimes left a twig with a leaf on it lying on the path. The broken end pointed in the right direction.

I have gone home A useful message if someone gets tired of the game! Make a ring of stones and put one in the middle.

Message near here Arrange four sticks in a square with one stone in the direction of the message. The number of paces away that the written message lies hidden should be shown by the number of stones inside the square.

I will be back soon A useful sign for campers. Push a stick into the ground and balance another stick across it, one end on the ground.

Water nearby This is an Indian sign. Use twigs to make a wavy pattern.

See if you can work out some more signs.

Setting up camp

Unless you are out in the wilds you cannot just set up a camp anywhere. All land belongs to someone. Even 'common' land, national parks and reserves have authorities in charge of them. Most have laws about camping and camp fires. Before pitching your tent and starting a campfire, ask permission. Land owners and authorities will say 'yes' if you look and sound as though you are sensible and will take care. In the wilds, of course, it is different. You can choose where you want to camp. But how will you decide on the right place?

Choosing a site
If you are setting up a camp for a stay of several days you will want somewhere where the view is pleasant. It is nicer for everyone if there is water nearby so that you can swim, row a boat or fish. If you are simply staying for one night and then moving on, the view does not matter so much. But there are some things which every campers should think about, whether the camp is for one night or several nights.
Trees first: it is a nice idea to pitch your tent under the protective branches of a big tree but it can be very uncomfortable and, sometimes, dangerous. If it rains, water will go on dripping onto your tent long after the rain has stopped. In winter, there is always the danger of falling branches or falling snow, although big trees will protect you from the wind. By all means put up your tent where trees can make shade during the middle of the day. It is a good idea to make sure that the sun is on the camp during the morning so that everything can be dried or aired.

*A well-arranged camp: pitch
tents out of the wind with food
stores under a ground sheet
nearby. The wood store is laid on
a couple of logs to keep it dry. A
latrine pit needs a screen if you
can make one. Dig a grease pit
and a rubbish pit, keeping the
turf green so that you can put it
back after you have filled the
holes when you leave the camp*

CAMPING OUT

Which direction?
Arrange the camp so that the tents face east or
south-east. Rain usually comes from the south-west
and west and it is better to face away from bad
weather.

Rocks make a very good wind breaks. Pitch
your tent near to big rocks that have been in the
sun all day. At night, you will be able to feel the
warmth seeping out of them. If you are camping in
hilly country, camp on the sheltered side of a hill,
out of the wind. If possible choose a place
immediately below a group of rocks or a clump of
trees. The cold air coming down from the top of the
hill will jump over the natural wind break and leave
you feeling much warmer.

Near to water
If you camp on a river bank look around first for
flood marks. You will be able to recognise these as
a thin line of rubbish, twigs and leaves and so on,
just above the waterline. Even if the flood mark is
old, camp above it to be quite sure. It is not wise to
camp on low ground at any time. The air is likely to
be damp and you will be plagued with mosquitos in
summer. Ravines and deep valleys are not wise
camp sites either because there is always the
possibility of mist in these places.

Putting up tents
Choose level ground for the tent site if possible. A
hillside is not going to be very comfortable for
anyone to sleep on and nor is a field which was
once ploughed. Even if the ground is now covered
in grass, those old furrows are going to feel like a
rolling sea of solid iron under a sleeping bag!

The worst ground for holding tent pegs is sand.
Clay is not much better. The safest ground for

Beds and blankets

putting up a tent is earth with some gravel in it. The soil holds the pegs firmly and, if it rains, the water soaks into the ground quickly. Bare earth is the safest surface for building camp fires.

Check on water first
But the most important thing every camp must have is water for drinking and cooking. Before you decide on a site, check on whether there is water near at hand and easy to collect.

Beds and blankets
Let us assume that you have got a little ridge tent of your own, big enough for two to sleep comfortably. Ideally, you would like to have proper sleeping bags and camp beds as well. But if you are only just starting to enjoy camping and sleeping out, perhaps all you have got is a couple of warm blankets each.

Lots of campers use just two blankets — in fact, many hunters prefer two blankets to sleeping bags. You can sleep warmly and comfortable with just blankets but the important thing you must have is a groundsheet. Never sleep on the bare ground. Some tents have a groundsheet all-in-one. If your tent has no groundsheet, carry one in your pack. Groundsheets are lightweight and you will find a great many uses for them.

Here are two ways of using the two blankets to make a bed. (Camp blankets should be soft and fluffy and, if possible, loosely woven).

Papoose bed
You need two blankets and three large blanket or safety pins. Lie down on blanket number 1. Fold blanket 2 down the middle and lay it over you, covering your head. Now hump your body in the air and tuck blanket 2 under your hips, under your legs

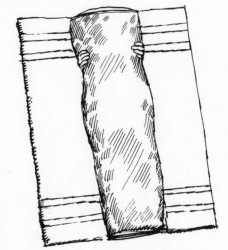

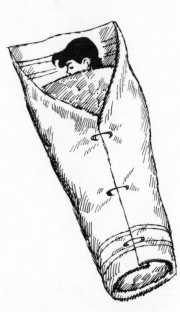

Papoose bed: tuck one blanket under you and pin the other round you

and round your feet. Fold the top of the blanket down so that it is level with your neck. Sit up and fold the bottom corners of blanket 2 across your feet. Pin the two layers together. Pin them again at your knee level. Draw the sides of blanket 1 across your middle and pin with the third pin.

Have a small pillow for your head for real comfort, but your folded clothes will do just as well. Your boots, laid down toe to toe, with your clothes folded on top will make a surprisingly comfortably head rest.

The papoose bed arrangement means that you have three layers of blanket over you and two under you. It is important to have at least two layers of blanket under your body if you are going to sleep warmly.

Hunter's bed
Again, you need two blankets and three large blanket or safety pins.

Arrange blanket 1 on the ground. Fold blanket 2 down the middle and lay it on blanket 1, to one side (see illustration). Fold the sides of blanket 1 to overlap and put in a pin to hold them. Fold up the foot and put in two pins. Slide into bed from the top. You have two layers of blanket on top of you and two under you. You are snugly pinned in at the bottom so that you cannot kick the blankets off in the night.

Next morning
Every morning, unless it is pouring with rain, shake out your blankets. Hang them on a tree or drape them over a rock to air before folding them into your pack. Leave blankets folded during the day if you are in camp. Unpeg the ground sheet and draw

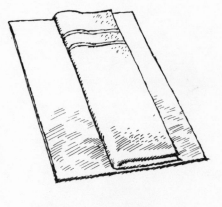

Hunter's bed: the bottom of the blankets are pinned to keep you from kicking them off

A healthy camp

it out of the tent so that the ground under it can dry during the day.

Sleeping clothes
When you are sleeping out, you can wear what you like during the night. Some people like to wear pyjamas and bed socks. Girls like to wear either pyjamas or nightgowns. But wear something, even if you usually sleep naked at home. Never sleep in anything that you have worn or intend to wear during the day. It is alright to have an old sweater with you and you can wear it instead of a pyjama top for warmth, but keep it just for night wearing.

A healthy camp
It is surprising how many people think that just because they are camping all the usual rules about cleanliness can be ignored. If you are in the wilds and water is in short supply, you might have to be careful about using fresh water for washing. But in normal circumstances, when water is easily obtained, everyone in camp should keep themselves as clean as possible. Apart from the fact that you will feel more comfortable, it is pleasanter for other people!

It is also important that all the things that you cook and eat with are washed and kept absolutely clean. If you are careless, flies will soon find scraps of food and grease on which to feed and lay their eggs. In no time at all, everyone will have a stomach upset and the holiday will be ruined.

Arranging the camp
Whether there are several tents or just one or two, the same basic rules apply in arranging the camp. The tents should be on level ground and to the leeward of where the cooking is going to be done.

(Leeward means that the wind will be blowing from
behind the tents towards the 'kitchen' area.) If you
are on your own in the wilds you will want your
camp fire fairly near to your tent so that you can
enjoy the warmth of it. But position the tent so that
the fire smoke blows away from the tent.

Have the wood pile near the fire. A short
distance from the cooking area, dig a rubbish pit
and a grease pit. Near to the tents (but not too
near), plan the latrine and the wash-place.

Latrine

Dig your latrine pit behind a bush or a rock, if
possible, so that people are not too embarrassed to
use it. Leave the pile of earth beside the hole with a
small shovel or a flat piece of wood. Then, after
using the pit, everyone shovels back some of the
earth. Hang a white cloth somewhere so that it can
be displayed and people can see when the latrine is
in use. If you are staying in camp for some time,
you might make a proper screen from sacking and a
few pieces of wood.

Grease pits and rubbish pits

Every spring, when the snows melt, the lower slopes
of Mount Everest turn into an enormous rubbish
dump! Tin cans, plastic bottles and food containers
of every kind have been left behind by the different
climbing teams who visit Nepal. It is a pity that the
Nepalese government cannot make a rule that
climbers must take their rubbish away with them!

Everyone who loves the countryside wants to
keep it looking beautiful. Rubbish left behind by
campers is not only unpleasant for everyone else but
it can also be dangerous to animals. Many wild
animals have been injured by nosing around sharp,
tin cans or have choked to death by eating food

Turfing

Lifting the turf from the soil with a spade edge

remains in plastic bags. Make it a rule that you will always bury all your camp rubbish, leaving the site just as you found it.

Dig two holes, one for rubbish and the other for a grease pit. If the ground is grassy, lift the grassy top layer off first and then you can put it back when you leave the camp. The grease pit is used for washing-up water. Dig it fairly deeply and lay branches or bracken across it to filter out the food bits. Pour the dirty water into the pit. Burn the filter branches every day and put in fresh ones.

Flatten empty tins and bury them with all your food scraps, vegetable peelings, egg shells etc. Bury plastic and glass bottles and empty spray cans. Burn paper on the camp fire.

Cover the rubbish pit with a sheet of plastic, weighted down with stones, to keep the flies out. Fill it in when you leave, putting the grass back on top.

Turfing

If you are camping in a national park or somewhere where the ground is grassed, you have to be even more careful about looking after the site. Grass gets damaged very easily and quickly shows the marks of a camp. Burned places take a long time to grow over again. When you dig holes, for a pit fire, a latrine or for rubbish, lift the grass off first. Here is how it is done.

What you need

You need a square-ended spade and a big sheet of polythene. Mark out the area of the hole you are going to dig, using the cutting edge of the spade. Cut down through the grass into the soil about 75mm (3in). Keep the spade blade upright as you dig down. Kneel down and work the edge of the

spade down into the soil and then under the grass.
Work along one side of the marked area until you
have loosened the grass roots from the soil.
Someone else should be ready to fold back the
grass. Gradually work under the grass from side to
side until you get to the end of the marked area.
Lift the rolled grass off the ground and take it to a
shady place, such as under a bush. Unroll it and lay
it grass-side up on the ground. Water the grass and
make sure that someone waters it every day to keep
it alive and growing. Now you can dig the hole.

Start in the middle of the patch of bare earth.
Lift spades of soil onto the polythene sheet. Dig the
hole as deep as you think you need it. Leave the
pile of soil on the polythene sheeting and near to
the hole with a trowel or a flat piece of wood
nearby so that rubbish etc., can be covered up as
the hole fills.

When you are ready to leave
Shovel as much of the soil back into the hole as
possible. Stamp it down firmly. Water the surface
and then lift the piece of grass from its shady place.
Position it on the bare earth and stamp it down.
Water it again and leave it.

Camping Gear

If you have never tried camping until now, you probably have very little of the equipment needed — even for an overnight sleep-out. You do not need a great deal. A tent is the most expensive item — and the most necessary. There are several different kinds and shapes to choose from. A simple ridge tent, which is about 125cm (4½ft) high by 150cm (5ft) wide and 200cm (7ft) long, is big enough for two or three young people.

With the tent you will get guy ropes and pegs for putting it up. You might even get a mallet thrown in too! If not, you need to buy one. It is used for knocking in the tent pegs.

You will need a groundsheet for the tent. These are sometimes all-in-one with the tent, and sometimes separate.

Each of you will need a sleeping bag or a pair of blankets.

Cooking in camp

The next priority is something to cook on. Camping shops sell small stoves fired with gas and these can be carried easily in a bicycle carrier. Or you may decide that you want to build a wood fire.

Pots and pans

You can take an old saucepan for cooking in if you really do not want to spend very much money but the billie cans sold by camping shops are best. They are lightweight and come in different sizes. Billies are shaped rather like paintpots with a handle so that they can be hung over the fire. You need at least two billies, one for cooking food and the other for heating water.

You also need a frying pan — non-stick if possible.

Other items

Here is a basic list of cooking equipment you might
need. Camping equipment becomes very much a
matter of personal taste. After one or two trips, you
will start to make up your own mind about what is
essential and what can be left behind. After all, you
have to carry it!

Billies
Frying pan
Big spoon (can be plastic)
Can opener
Sharp cook's knife
Bread knife
Basin and a small jug
Folding container for carrying water
Plastic containers for carrying basic foods
Tin foil
Plastic bags
Toilet paper

For washing up

Bowl or basin
Detergent liquid in plastic bottle
Scouring pad, dish mop
2 drying cloths

Personal equipment

Spare items of clothing, toilet articles, soap, sponge
or face cloth, towel, toothbrush and toothpaste etc.,
Each member of the camp team should also take a
tin or plastic plate, a shallow bowl (for soup, cereal
or pudding), a mug, and a knife, fork and spoon. A
good flashlight and a strong pocket knife are useful
extras.

Quartermaster's stores

One person should be responsible for the stores. Otherwise something is certain to be left behind. Make a list together and then leave it to the quartermaster.

The essential stores are:
Candles and matches*
Cord, sisal or rope
Axe for chopping wood (if you are planning to build a fire).
Something to dig with, such as a small spade or a trowel.

*Here is an old woodman's tip for your matches. Choose the non-safety kind because they will strike on anything rough. If the weather is likely to be wet, waterproof the matches before you set off. Melt a candle-end in a tin can over hot water. Pour the melted candle wax over the box of matches so that all the sticks are coated. When you need a match break it out of the wax. The matches stay dry and the wax coating helps the match to burn longer.

Food stores

Start off by writing down everything you know you can cook or prepare. If you can peel and boil potatoes, or fry sausages, eggs and bacon, you know right away the kind of food you could manage in camp. Base your planned meals on what you know you can cook.

There are some very good 'convenience' foods in the shops which make life easy for a camper. Many need only water added before cooking to make a nourishing and appetizing meal. Take along a selection of these dry-packs. They are usually packed in foil or flat card boxes and take up very little space.

Tins are generally too heavy to be worth carrying. Buy tinned food locally. Tinned food is a

Camp cooking

good standby when the weather is bad. You have
only to open the can, heat it over a candle in a can,
(see illustration), and then eat from the can.

How much food?
People get very hungry in camp. They eat far more
than they do at home. Be prepared for enormous
quantities of food to be eaten. Plan to eat breakfast,
a snack mid-morning, lunch, tea, supper and a
before-bed snack.
The basic foods: Do not leave any of these behind.
Salt, pepper, beef stock cubes, tea bags (or
powdered coffee if you drink it), milk powder,
sugar, butter, cooking fat and flour.

Camp cooking
Camp meals should be easy to prepare and, if
possible, cooked in only one or two pots. Breakfast
will be a fry-up because everyone likes eggs and
bacon when they are eating outdoors! You can eat
some cereal too if you like it or, if the mornings are
a bit chilly and misty, make a billie of hot, creamy
porridge! Served with a big spoonful of brown
sugar, it is a good start to the day.

At mid-morning, everyone will want to stop for
a break if they are in camp. Have a drink of some
kind — cocoa, tea or fruit squash — and a
chocolate cookie or biscuit. Lunch can be a light
meal because you will be having a campfire feast
later when it gets dark. It is quite a good idea to
have a cold meal at midday and start doing the
vegetables and so on for the evening meal later.
Mid-afternoon, another break with a hot drink and
buttered toast or a slice of cake. And then the high
spot of the day, hot supper with everyone sitting
round the campfire. This is the best time of all and
you can eat a delicious hunter's stew, cooked in a

large billie or grill pieces of chicken over the coals. Finish supper with an easy sweet, such as a quick-mix milk pudding, fresh fruit or chocolate.

Here are some tried and tasted camp food recipes.

Breakfast porridge
A small handful of dry oats for each person. Leave the oats to soak overnight in a little cold water. Next morning, put in a pinch of salt, add milk (or milk powder mixed with water). Stir the porridge over a gentle fire until thick, adding more milk as you need it. Serve hot with sugar, and milk if liked.

Eggs and bacon
Warm the frying pan over the fire. Cut the rinds from the bacon. Chop them up and put in the frying pan with some cooking fat — not much, about a small spoonful. When the fat melts, lay the bacon in the pan. Arrange the bacon so that the fatty part of each piece is touching the bottom of the pan with the meat part of the next slice lying on the fat of the first. This makes sure that the fat cooks properly without the meat getting overdone. Fry the bacon until the fat is crisp. Lift it out and put it on a tin plate near to the fire, covered with another plate. Put some more fat in the frying pan. Let it melt. Break an egg into a mug. To do this, bang the egg on the side of the cup to dent the shell. Break the eggshell open on the dent, with the thumbs of both hands. Pour the egg into the hot fat. Several eggs can go in together. When the white part is cooked the eggs are done. Divide them with a knife blade. Serve with the bacon.

Sausages Prick sausages all over with a fork before frying or grilling them. It prevents the skins from bursting.

Kidneys Cut kidneys in half, skin them and cut out the fatty middle. Fry.

Chips Peel potatoes. Cut into thick slices. Cut each slice into thin sticks. Dry on a cloth. Fry in hot fat.

Saute potatoes Boil some big potatoes. Let them get cold. Slice them and fry.

Scrambled eggs Break eggs into a basin. Allow two eggs for each person. Stir them up a little. Add a pinch of salt and a shake of pepper. Melt some butter in the frying pan. As soon as it is melted, pour in the eggs. Stir over a slow, gentle fire until the eggs are just set. Serve with hot toast.

Poached eggs

Put some water in the frying pan. Add a teaspoon of salt. Let the water get hot. When it starts to bubble, break an egg into a cup and pour into the water. It will set immediately. Lift the pan off the fire a little so that the water just simmers. In two or three minutes the egg will be cooked. Lift it out with a big spoon. Tip the spoon to let the water drain off. Plop the egg onto a piece of buttered toast.

Welsh Rarebit Grate some cheese. Heat a mug of milk in a billie can. Beat up one egg with a fork. Add the cheese to the hot milk and then stir in the egg. Salt and pepper. When the cheese has melted, take the billie from the fire and add a knob of butter. Stir and serve on hot toast. Welsh Rarebit can also be served by putting it all in one dish. Everyone scoops up the rarebit with sticks of toast or bits of damper (see page 75).

Cheese fries Cut two slices of bread, butter them and make a cheese sandwich. Cut it in half. Beat up an egg. Dip the sandwiches in the egg on both sides. Fry both sides until brown.

Pancakes You can buy pancake mix and simply add milk. If you cannot get this, make pancake mix as follows. Measure four big spoons of flour into a bowl. Break in one egg. Stir and then slowly add a mug of water and milk mixed. There should not be any lumps. The mixture should be smooth and not too thick. Pour the mixture into a jug.

Sweet Pancakes Add a spoonful of sugar to the pancake mix. Melt some cooking fat in a pan. Pour in enough of the mix to just cover the bottom of the pan. Tilt the pan to make it run to the sides. Fry gently. With a knife, turn the pancake over. When the pancake is cooked, life it onto a hot plate. Put a spoonful of jam on the pancake, fold it over and serve with cream and sugar. A good, hot pudding.

Savoury pancakes Add a pinch of salt and some pepper to the mix. (No sugar in a savoury pancake). Fry in exactly the same way as for the sweet pancake. Spoon chopped ham, peas, cooked mushrooms, bits of cooked chicken etc. on the pancake. Fold over and serve with tomato ketchup.

Potato cakes Make up some potato mix with water. Let the mashed potato get cold so that it is thick enough to handle. Using your hands, roll balls of the mashed potato and then flatten them into rounds. Fry in hot fat on both sides. Good with bacon or with cold ham.

Bubble and Squeak This is a good way of using up any cooked vegetables that are left over. Chop up some cooked potato. Melt some fat in the frying pan. Spoon in the chopped potato and then spoon cooked cabbage or mashed-up brussells sprouts on top. More potato goes on top. Fry until the potato is brown and then turn the whole cake over and brown the other side. This is good to eat as it is but is fantastic with fried bacon!

Spaghetti and sauce You can get very good
spaghetti meat sauce in dry-packs which are mixed
with water before cooking, or ready-to-heat in tins.
Spaghetti comes in long sticks. Break the sticks in
half. Boil a big billie of water. Add a spoonful of
salt. When the water is boiling and bubbling, stand
the spaghetti sticks in the water. As the spaghetti
softens, it will slide to the bottom of the billie. Help
it down by pushing with a spoon. Let it boil and
cook. Lift out one piece of spaghetti with a fork to
see if the spaghetti is cooked. It should take about
15 minutes. Pour off the hot water. Add a knob of
butter, serve with hot spaghetti sauce.

You can also serve spaghetti with butter and
grated cheese or, try it the Italian way. Fry some
bacon very crisply. Break into bits. Beat up three
eggs. Stir the eggs into the buttered spaghetti over
the fire. Last, add the crumbled bacon and serve.
Macaroni can be cooked and served in the same
ways.

Camp breads
Even if bread is easy to buy locally, try and make
some camp bread as well.

Dampers These are made in the frying pan and are
as good as new bread to eat. Put two large handfuls
of self-raising (cake) flour into a basin. Add two
teaspoons of baking powder and a pinch of salt.
Mix with cold water to make a stiff dough. Heat
some fat in a frying pan. Break off pieces of dough
and make balls. Then flatten the balls by pulling the
sides out. The damper should be about 10mm ($\frac{1}{4}$in
thick). Put the damper in the pan and hold it over
the fire. The dough will puff up. Now take the pan
off the fire and stand it, leaning against a stone, so
that the fire grills the top of the damper. When it is
brown, turn the damper over, grill the other side.

Twisters
You need some green sticks for spits. Cut some
sticks about 25mm (1in) thick. Peel the bark off and
then heat the sticks over the fire. Make the same
dough mixture as for the dampers. Break lumps and
roll them into coils between your hands. Wind the
coils round the hot, green sticks. Hold them over
the fire to brown. You can test if twisters are
cooked by sticking a knife tip into the dough. If it
comes out without sticky dough on it, the twisters
are ready to eat.

Scones
Add a little sugar and a few currants to the damper
mixture. Heat the frying pan and put in a little fat.
Roll balls and then flatten them into rounds about
10mm ($\frac{1}{2}$in) thick. Cook gently on both sides. Eat
hot with butter and jam.

Flapjacks
Make the same damper mixture but add more water
to make a batter. Fry flapjacks in the same way as
pancakes.

Camp cooking tip: If you want to mix foods
together, such as when you are making camp bread
dough, you can use a plastic bag instead of a basin
or bowl and save washing up. Put all the ingredients
into the plastic bag and tie the neck. Squeeze the
bag to mix everything together.

Rabbit for supper!

Cooking rabbit
A rabbit can be cooked whole after skinning and cleaning. Here are two ways of roasting a whole rabbit.

Speared rabbit
Cut a green stick and sharpen both ends to make a spit. Push the stick in and out through the loose skin under the ribs of the rabbit. It should hang quite securely from the spit. Build a good fire and rake the coals to one side of the fire. Rest the spit across two wooden forks over the coals. Turn the rabbit as it roasts. Rake more coals out as the fire burns to keep the roasting going. (Do not try and roast over a fire that is making smoke. It will blacken the meat and spoil the taste.) Stick a fork in the meat to see if it is done.

Rabbit in tin foil
Tear off two large pieces of tinfoil. Lay them, edges overlapping, and use as one sheet. Rub fat on the surface and lay the rabbit on the foil. Chop some carrot and an onion. Sprinkle the vegetables on the rabbit. Add some mixed herbs if you have them. Salt and pepper the meat. Add a lump of butter or a piece of fat bacon. Fold the foil over the rabbit. Fold the edges of the parcel on all three sides so that it is completely sealed. Lay the foil parcel directly on the coals and leave it to cook for about an hour. Turn the parcel over two or three times. You can also cook pieces of rabbit in the same way.

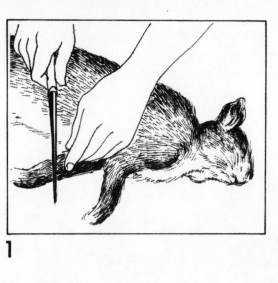

1

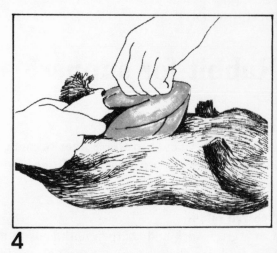

4

2

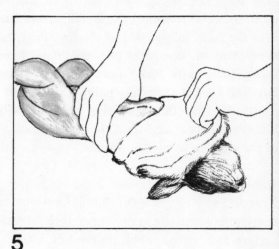

5

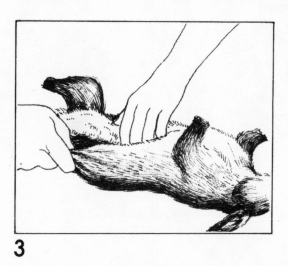

3

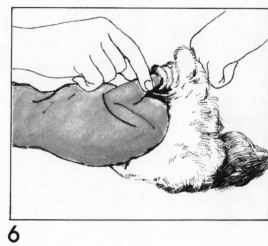

6

All good woodsmen know how to skin a rabbit. Do not be queasy about it. A rabbit is good food and you should know how to prepare one for the stewpot. Here is how to skin and prepare a rabbit, step-by-step.

1. Lay the rabbit on a piece of newspaper and cut off the feet at the first joint, using a sharp, short-bladed knife.
2. Lay the rabbit on its back and slit up the belly from between the back legs to between the forelegs. Cut through the fur and skin only. Do not cut right down into the flesh.
3. Put your fingers between the fur and flesh and you will find that you can ease the skin away quite easily. Peel the skin back from the body on both sides.
4. Now pull the skin off the hind legs.
5. Pull the skin towards the head. Ease the fur off the front legs.
6. Now the fur is up on the neck. Cut the rabbit's head off with a sharp knife.
7. Before the rabbit can be cooked, the insides have to be taken out. Cut right up the belly with scissors or a knife. Take out everything inside the body with your fingers. Now the rabbit can be cut into pieces.
8. Cut the body in half along the length. Cut off the fore legs. Cut off the hind legs. Cut the body into two or three pieces. Wash the meat carefully in cold water before cooking.

Hunter's Stew

A rich hunter's stew can be made with any kind of meat as well as with rabbit. Give a stew about 2 hours to cook properly.

Equipment you need: frying pan, sharp knife, jug for water, stirring spoon, teaspoon, big cooking pot with a lid.

Food you need: meat, potatoes, onions, carrots, cooking fat, salt and pepper, a little sugar. Flour if you like a thick stew. Beef or chicken stock cube for more flavour.

1   Cut the meat into squares or the rabbit into pieces.

2   Put some flour on a plate. Add a teaspoon of salt and pepper. Roll the meat in the flour.

3   Put the frying pan on the fire. Put in a lump of cooking fat. Let it melt and get hot.

4   Put the meat into the fat and let it brown. Turn the pieces over. Meanwhile, slice an onion. Take the browned meat out with a spoon and put it into the big cooking pot.

5   Put the sliced onion into the frying pan with a little more fat if it is needed. Let the onion cook. Add a spoonful of sugar. Stir everything up.

6   Pour some water into the frying pan and stir again so that all the browned bits come off the bottom of the frying pan. Pour the water and onions into the big cooking pot.

7   Mix a stock cube with some more water and pour it over the meat. The meat should be completely covered with water. Add some more water if necessary. Put the cooking pot on the fire and cook the meat for an hour.

8   Meanwhile, peel and cut up the vegetables. Taste the gravy in the stewpot to see if it needs any more salt and pepper. Add the vegetables and let the stew cook for another hour.

Camp fires

There are good reasons for knowing how to make camp fires. For one thing, if you are on a trek, a camp stove and its fuel is extra weight to carry. Also, a camp stove is not much good for drying wet clothes or making a signal light for people away from the camp. But anyway, what could be more cheerful after a day's walking than sitting round a proper camp fire with the flames flickering and a smell of woodsmoke?

Warnings first

If you have ever seen a forest or heath fire, you know how terrible they can be. The flames rush across the ground and leap from tree to tree, destroying everything in their path. Animals and birds lose their homes and, sometimes, their lives. The blackened, scarred ground left after a fire sometimes takes as many as twenty years to recover and grow green plants again. No one who is sensible wants to be the cause of this kind of destruction. It is not only foolish to be careless with fire in the countryside, it is criminal, so read the next bit very carefully and remember all of it always.

Fire sense

On state land and in national parks there is usually a law saying that fires can only be built in pits or holes. Find out the laws of the camping land first. If you are on private land, you must ask permission from the owner before starting a fire.

Choose a place in the open without trees hanging overhead and away from bushes. If the weather is very windy, it is safer to build your fire against a rock but if there are none, make sure the tents or shelters are a good distance away.

Clear a place for the fire. Scrape away dead leaves and pine needles, right down to the bare

earth. If the ground is turfed, try and lift the turf off the ground so that you can put it back when you leave. Cut long grass very short.

Keep your camp fire fairly small. Big fires are more likely to get out of control. Heap your firewood a short distance away or a flying spark may catch fire to it and you will have two fires going and be in trouble! Keep some water handy for emergencies.

Lastly, when you have finished with the fire and you are breaking camp, let the fire die right down and then drench it with water. Stir the ashes to make sure that there is not a spark left anywhere and then to make quite sure, smother the whole fire site with earth or sand.

When you are lighting fires, put the match end into the fire. Get into the habit of doing this. Do not simply toss it over your shoulder because the match could land in dry leaves and then smoulder into flames.

Forest fires have sometimes been started because a camper has left a piece of broken glass on dry leaves. The sun's rays through the glass can strike fire so always collect bottles together and take them with you or, at least, bury them in the earth.

Indian know-how
There is an old American Indian saying, 'White man fool, he make big fire and not get near. Injun make little fire and get close!' American Indians knew all about camping and were good backwoodsmen and this saying makes a lot of sense. There is no point in building a great big, roaring fire if you cannot get near enough to put a cooking pot on it.

If you want to be a good backwoodsman, be comfortable and not spend all your time looking for firewood, learn how to make the right kind of fire

Tinder and kindling

for the job. Some fires are made for a quick brew-up. Others are best for frying or for roasting food. And it is good to know how to make a good, warming camp fire to sit round.

To make a good fire you start with tinder. This is stuff that catches fire easily such as dead bramble, dry bracken, weed stalks, dry fir cones, birch and cedar bark from fallen trees. Birch is particularly good if you have only one match — it flares up when it is lit. Twigs which are lying on the ground are usually too damp.

Next, gather the kindling. This can be dry tree bark again together with sticks and twigs broken from the dead part of trees and bushes.

Finally, gather the firewood. To store firewood, lay two sticks side by side and about 30cm (12in) apart and lay the rest of the firewood across it.

Here are some verses to learn about the best woods for burning.

Oak logs will warm you well
If they're old and dry
Larch logs of pine woods smell
But the sparks will fly.

Beech logs for Christmas-time
Yew logs heat well
'Scotch' logs it is a crime
For anyone to sell.

Birch logs will burn too fast
Chestnut scarce at all
Hawthorne logs are good to last
If cut at the fall.

Indian fire

Holly logs will burn like wax
You should burn them green
Elm logs like smouldering flax
No flame to be seen.

Pear logs and apple logs
They will scent the room
Cherry logs across the dogs will
Smell like flowers in bloom.

But ash logs all smooth and grey
Burn them green or old
Buy up all that come your way
They're worth their weight in gold.

*Start an Indian fire
with three sticks in a
wigwam shape*

Now you know the best types of wood for making a fire and you are ready to build one.

One word of warning   That fourth line in the first verse is true not only of larches, but also of elder wood, red cedar, hemlock, balsam, spruce and all of the soft pinewoods. Fires made of these woods spit sparks so be careful where you make your camp.

Indian Fire
First, push a forked stick into the ground and pile tinder round it. Choose three kindling sticks as thick as a finger and, with a penknife blade, shave the bark and the wood into curls about one half of the length. Stand these sticks round the forked stick, the curls hanging downwards. Stand more kindling sticks round to make a wigwam shape. Leave spaces between the sticks because fires need a lot of air to help them to burn. When the fire is ready, squat facing the wind, strike the match and set it to the tinder. Throw the match end into the fire. As the fire burns the kindling, add more sticks

Hunter's fire

to the wigwam. In about twenty minutes you will
have a good fire going.

In wet, windy weather, it is quite a test of your
woodsmanship to make and light a camp fire. To
light the match, squat **facing** the wind holding the
match cupped in one hand and the other hand
completing the cup with the match held between the
fingers and thumb, the head pointing away from
you. Strike the match and immediately resume the
cup shape made by the hands. The flame will run
up the matchstick instead of away from it and thus
stay alight.

Camp fires for cooking
You do not need a large fire to make a hot drink or
a quick meal. The Indian fire burns up quickly and
will be ready to cook on in about 20 minutes. You
will need something to hang up your cooking pot or
kettle. You can make what is called a 'camp crane'.

Camp crane
Drive a forked stick into the ground. If you cannot
find a forked stick, cut a notch in a straight stick.
Look for a long, green stick (green means the stick
still has some sap in it) and rest it in the fork with
one end on the ground. The end in the air should
have a stub of twig on it to hold the handle of the
pot or kettle but if it has none, cut another notch.
Lay a heavy rock on the other end of the stick.
Hang the kettle or cooking pot on the twig. It
should hang about 300mm (12in) above the ground.
You can alter the height by moving the end with the
rock on it. Now build your fire under the pot.

Hunter's fire
A good backwoodsman does not waste a fire once
he has it going. Let us suppose that you have built

*A camp crane holds the cooking pot
over the flames*

Lumberman's fire

your fire and you are heating some soup or some water for a hot drink. You are thinking about some fried sausages and eggs for your supper. While the water is coming to a boil, look for two thick pieces of wood about 130mm (5in) thick and 450mm (18in) long or two flattish stones. After the kettle or pot has boiled, the fire will start to die down. Lay the two pieces of wood on each side of the fire, close enough so that they will support a frying pan. Rake out any smoking pieces of wood and start your fry-up over the hot, red embers.

Lumberman's fire

Lumbermen sometimes have to be out all night in very cold, sometimes freezing weather and they want to keep the fire going all night, not just for warmth in the camp but so that they have a fire ready to cook some breakfast the next morning.

Get two thick bed logs first — as thick as you can find them. Lay them side by side as shown in the illustration. The ends are about 400mm (16in) apart at one end and 200mm (8in) apart at the other. Lay green, sappy sticks across the log platform and then build your fire on the sticks. Add firewood to get the fire going, laying the wood in a criss-cross fashion. You can make cooking pot supports as shown in the picture or rest the cooking pots on the logs.

After you have had your meal and enjoyed the fire, get it ready for the night. The wood burned through the evening will have dropped down between the logs and the insides of these will also have started to burn. Lay two thick green logs across the bed logs and heap more firewood on top. Someone will probably have to feed the fire during the night but in really cold weather it is good to have the warmth and glow of the fire so it is worth

A lumberman's fire is made to last all night so that breakfast can be quickly prepared the next morning

Pitfire for stewpots

the trouble. In the morning, the coals will be hot and red and you can start cooking breakfast right away.

Lazy camp fire

Sometimes you need a fire that is going to burn very slowly and not need too much attention. A star-shaped fire is just the thing. Lay three pieces of wood in a triangle and then build an Indian fire inside it. When you have got a blaze going, push fairly thick pieces of wood into the heart of the fire so that the ends radiate round the fire like a star. As the wood burns away, push the sticks into the fire. You only need about 5 or 6 thick sticks to make a good fire for your camp.

Pit fire for stewpots

You will probably want to fry most of your camp food. Frying is certainly the quickest and easiest way of getting a hot meal ready. But in cold weather there is nothing so good to eat as a rich, tasty stew.

A stew takes at least two hours to cook properly so the fire has to be long-lasting. A pit fire is the answer. Clear the ground of pine needles, dead leaves and so on. Dig a trench about 60cm (24in) long with one end about 200mm (8in wide) and the other end about 300mm (12in wide). The narrow end should be towards the wind. The trench should be shallow at the windward end — about 150mm (6in) deep and much deeper at the wide end.

Put some flat stones at the bottom of the hole. Arrange rocks round the trench edge with one big flat stone over the narrow end. Look at the illustration. Build an Indian fire in the deep end of the fire pit. When it is burning well, lean thick sticks against the sides of the hole with the ends in

Build an Indian fire at the deep end

Underground oven

the fire. Hang the stewpot over the flames. As the wood burns down, the embers fall into the bottom of the hole. Soon there is a good hot bed of coals to keep the stewpot simmering. You can build a pit fire, start the supper going and go for a long walk while it cooks. A pit fire is the best fire for windy weather too. The sloping floor of the trench makes a good draught without the wind putting out the flames.

Underground oven

Many country cooks know about cooking in a hay box. A hay box is a big wooden box with a lid. The bottom and sides of the box and the inside of the lid are covered with a thick layer of hay. When a hot pot of food is put into the haybox and the lid fastened down, the heat cannot escape through the hay. This is called 'insulating' the pot. The pot stays almost as hot as it was when it was put into the box and the food goes on cooking.

You can do this kind of cooking in camp. You could start the supper stew at lunch time and leave it simmering all afternoon.

Building the oven

You need a pot with a close-fitting lid. Dig a hole in the ground three times as wide as the pot and three times as deep. Gather a lot of dried leaves, dried grasses, bracken etc., and line the hole, leaving just enough space for the cooking pot in the middle. More dried stuff will be piled on top of the pot when it is inside the hole. Pack the dried stuff down as firmly as you can.

Prepare the stew and start it cooking over the camp fire. Let it bubble for about half an hour and then, without taking off the lid, lift the pot immediately into the hole. Hold it carefully with a

An underground oven keeps a pot of food hot because the air cannot get to it through the leaves and grass in the hole

cloth because it can burn you. Quickly pile the rest of the dry leaves and bracken on top of pot and push some down the sides as well. The tighter the packing, the better the result will be. Finally, put a piece of plastic sheeting over the top of the oven and hold it down with big stones and rocks. When you are ready to eat, several hours later, the food should be cooked and piping hot. If you want to use the oven again, protect it from rain by laying the plastic sheet over the top of the hole.

Old smokey

This is a good idea from Canada and useful for when you are camping near to water. There are always flying insects near water and some of them bite. A smokey can help to keep insects away from the camp. Pierce holes round the bottom edge of a large can. Put a few hot embers from the camp fire in the bottom and heap green leaves and twigs on top. The greenery will smoulder and make a lot of smoke. Stand the can windward of the camp so that the smoke blows towards you. The smell is not unpleasant and it certainly helps to keep the insects away from your camp.

The smoke from smouldering twigs and leaves, stuffed into a tin can, will help to keep flying insects away from the camp

Indian shelters

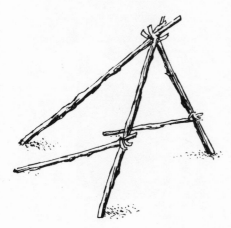

To camp properly, you must have a tent of some kind and learn how to use it. You might enjoy sleeping out on warm nights with just a sleeping bag but this is not camping and anyway, you would probably not want to do it all the time.

For a day's camping, it is fun to be able to make a shelter of some kind from branches and bracken or grasses. A 'green den' makes a good hide for watching birds and animals too.

Making a green den

Find three long branches, one a bit longer than the other two and roughly 150cm—180cm (5—6ft) long. If there is a natural fork at the end of each so much the better. The forks will interlock and hold without tying. Otherwise, tie the three branch ends together with a diagonal lashing. (See page 105). Arrange the branches like the picture to make a frame.

If you were out in a big forest and you were making a shelter for the night, you would cover the frame with branches of spruce or larch, in a kind of thatch. In 'soft' country, lean more branches against the main pole and then make a thatch of bracken or long grasses and reeds. Built in this way, a green den will hold two people sitting down. You can make it larger for more people by adding two more side poles, as in the picture. This makes the den rounded at the back and gives you more space. If you liked, you could make your den weatherproof by putting an old ground sheet over the frame instead of making a thatch.

Make a shelter from branches and greenery. It can be big enough for two or, with extra side poles, will hold more people

90

Bivouacs

The word bivouac (pronounce it biv-oo-ack) means a shelter you use for a little while but not a proper tent. It can be made of branches and leaves — like the green den — or it can be made of a material of some kind. If the material is waterproofed, a bivouac makes a good substitute for a one-night sleep-out in summer.

A bivouac can be made in all kinds of ways, depending where you are and what you have available.

In a garden, two trees and a laundry line will do. Throw a ground sheet over the line and weight it down at the sides with big stones. In the countryside, you might tie one end of a rope to a young tree and peg the other end to the ground. Probably the easiest and quickest bivouac to make is one using a low wall — just the thing if you get caught out in a heavy fall of rain!

A rope tied to a young tree and a ground sheet will make a quick shelter if the weather gets bad

Bedding down in a bivouac

Tents usually have a ground sheet inside them so that the damp and cold does not rise up and freeze the occupants during the night! But suppose you were a hunter out in a forest and you had to make a shelter for the night. You could make yourself a bivouac of some kind and, if you wanted to be sure of a good nights sleep, you'd make yourself a bed too using soft, springy greenery. Spruce and larch trees have suitable green or you could use bracken or ferns but you need a great deal to make a soft bed. Lay some sticks down first, criss-crossing them. Pile the bracken or ferns on top. Climb into the greenery so that you have a good layer beneath you and another layer over you.

Water first!

The most important thing a camp site must have is pure water to drink and cook with. Proper camping grounds usually have fresh water nearby. If you were camping on private land the owner would probably let you have water from a tap or faucet. But in the wilds, water is not nearly so easy to find. Even in forests and woods where everything is green there may not be pure water.

Be careful!

Some people think that running water, such as a stream or a river, must be fresh and safe to drink. This may not always be true. You do not know what is happening further upstream. There may be a dead animal in the water! Dead and rotting animal matter poisons the water and, if you drink it, it will poison you. Animal matter does not only mean dead animals. It means the bodies of fish and birds too.

Poison can also get into water from the drains of houses and farms on the river banks. The waste from drains is called sewage and many rivers and lakes have sewage flowing into them through sewage pipes. Unless you are quite sure that there are no houses or farms on the river or lake side, do not trust the water.

Dead and rotting vegetable matter in water is rather different. Vegetable matter is anything that has been growing — the leaves from trees, plants, grasses, water weed, reeds and so on. A pool with dead vegetable matter in it would look slimy and very unpleasant. It would smell awful and be revolting to drink. But if an explorer were very desperate he might have to drink from a stagnant pool to stay alive. By boiling the water for a long time, he could make it safe to drink.

Boiling pond water

To make it safe to drink, water has to be kept boiling for at least half an hour. Put handfuls of charcoal from the camp fire into the water as it boils. Charcoal is the black crumbly stuff left when wood has burned. Charcoal helps to make the water taste better when it has cooled.

As the water boils, a scum will come to the top. Skim this off with a plate or saucer. Put some fresh charcoal into the water and leave it overnight before using it.

The safest water
A spring of water, coming out of rock, is the safest water to drink. Underground streams can often be trusted too. Trail your hand in the water along the river bank or lake side. You may suddenly find a place where the water is much colder. This is an underground stream flowing in. Dig a deep hole about 1m (1 yard) back from the bank. You will probably find the stream. Scoop up the water as it bubbles into the hole. It may be muddy but muddy water can be cleared enough to make it drinkable.

Clearing muddy water
Quite a lot of the mud will settle to the bottom if the water is left standing overnight. Pour off the water into a clean pot. If you are in a hurry you can filter the muddy water through a piece of cloth.
If nothing else is available, a bunch of grass makes a good filter too. Tie the ends of a big bunch of grasses. Stand the bunch in a clean pot and pour the muddy water through.

The next stage needs a precipitate. This is a powder that will sink to the bottom taking the dissolved mud with it, leaving the water clear. Chalk is the best precipitate and your camp may have some nearby.

Making drinking water

Cornflour or cornmeal will also act as precipitates and so will dried oats. Put a good handful of one of these into a litre (2 pints) of water and leave for an hour or two. The water will almost clear and you can drink it. You can certainly cook with it, but it would make rather nasty coffee or tea. However you cannot have everything in the backwoods!

Making drinking water

Supposing you were lost somewhere where there was no water. Perhaps in the desert or in scrub land. The sun would be very hot and you would have to have water to stay alive while you were waiting to be rescued. What would you do?

You might find an underground stream by digging under a growing bush. You could get a little water every day by licking the dew off everything in camp in the early morning. You might also make a pit still. Try making one on the next hot day and see how well it works.

You need a ground sheet or a large piece of polythene sheeting. Spread the sheet on the ground and mark out an area a bit smaller. Put away the ground sheet and dig a deep hole. The deeper the hole is the more likely you are to get damp soil. About 120cm — 150cm (4—5ft) deep, will do. Stand a large can or pot in the hole in the middle. Arrange green leaves or bunches of grass or bracken round the can and up the sides of the hole. Lay the ground sheet over the top. Make quite sure that none of the green branches are touching the ground sheet anywhere. Arrange large rocks and stones all round the edge to hold the ground sheet down firmly and to make the hole as airtight as possible. Put one small stone in the middle of the sheet

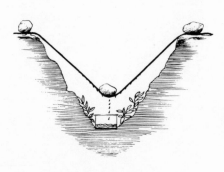

Try making a still in the ground on the next hot day. Fill the hole with greenery but it should not touch the cover

carefully, directly over the hidden can. Look at the illustration. During the day, the hot sun will draw up any water which is in the ground and from the green leaves. The water will turn into water vapour — something like the steam that comes off boiling water. This is called evaporation. You must not disturb the ground sheet at all or the water vapour will escape. When night comes and the air gets cooler, the surface of the ground sheet gets cold.

As the water vapour touches the cold ground sheet, it turns into tiny droplets of water. The droplets run down the sloping sides of the ground sheet and drip into the can in the middle of the hole. You have made fresh, clean drinking water from damp soil and greenery. A pot of dirty water put into the pit still would evaporate in the same way.

You can try another experiment with an ordinary plastic bag which will show you that even the air in your lungs has water in it. Blow into the plastic bag and fill it with your breath. Tie the neck tightly to knot it. Hang the bag outdoors in the sun and leave it overnight. In the morning, the inside of the bag will be covered with tiny drops of water. Some will have collected at the bottom of the bag.

Water from snow
You might suppose that if there was snow round your camp you would not be short of water. After all snow is frozen water and all you have to do is melt it! But it is not quite as easy as that. If you were to take a lump of snow, put into a frying pan and heat it over the fire the snow would melt all right but very slowly. The small amount of water would quickly evaporate over the heat. You would finish up with an empty pan and no water! To make snow into water you have to start with a little

Survival camp

water. If there is none, take a little piece of snow into the tent or where it is warmer and let it melt naturally. Then add small lumps of snow and gently heat it over the fire. Add more snow gradually until you have enough water.

After you have had two or three camping trips, try 'survival' camping, just once. It is worth testing yourself to see how little you actually need. There is no need to go miles away to make a survival camp. The backyard will do or a field just down the road. The important thing is that you use as little equipment as possible and see if you can actually find some of your food!

Survival camp

You do not have to sleep out, unless the weather is very warm and you really want to. Make a shelter for the day — a green den or a bivouac (page 91). Carry some water to your camp in a jar and make it last all day. Go carefully with it as though you had to climb two miles up a steep hill to get more!

Light a fire in a hole (page 87) so that your wood lasts a long time. Cook a rabbit over the fire, either roasting it or by grilling. Cut pieces of the meat and spear the bits on green twigs. Roast a potato in foil on the coals. Or cover the potato with a layer of mud and cook it in the same way.

You can cook a fish in foil on the coals or you could try wrapping it in wet, green leaves. The important thing is that the fire must be kept away from the fish's skin.

Supposing you had a wood pigeon or a small chicken to cook! Pull the feathers off first. Pull them against the way they grow. Hang up the bird so that all the blood runs into the head. Cut the head off and cut a hole just under the tail. Put your

fingers in and pull out all the insides. Spear the bird
on a green stick and grill it over a hot fire. Eat the
meat straight from the stick, using your fingers.

Supposing your survival camp is on a beach.
There might be shellfish about that you could eat.
Now you have to be very careful. There is an old
saying that you should never eat shellfish unless
there is an 'r' in the month. This is true in the
northern hemisphere because all the autumn, winter
and spring months have an 'r' in them, (September
to April). South of the equator, the old saying does
not hold true. The truth is that shellfish should not
be eaten in the hot summer months. Never eat
shellfish that appear to be dead. Gather them after
the tide has gone out when they are fastened to
rocks or are bubbling in the sand. Leave shellfish in
a clean pool of water until you are ready to use
them. Plunge shellfish straight into boiling water
and let them cook.

Catching fish
If your camp is on a lake side or on the sea shore,
you can pass the time fishing. You might be able to
catch a fish you can eat for supper and then you
will have achieved something very important in
survival. You will have found some food!

The easiest way
Netting is the easiest way to catch fish on the sea
shore. Two people take ends of a long net. An old
trawling net is the best but you could use a length
of a thin, open weave fabric such as muslin. Weight
the bottom edge with stones tied into the edge of
the fabric with string. Tie cork floats to the top edge.
One person stands in the shallows. The other wades
out into deeper water. The deepwater fisherman
begins to walk backwards to the shore pulling the

Spear fishing

net towards him as he walks. The shallows fisherman walks slowly along the shore but stops when the deepwater fisherman begins to get near the shore. Both pull, drawing together, to the beach. If there are fish in the shallows, you will net them in.

A fish-catching spear to make from pieces of wood

Spear fishing

This is great fun to do, but takes some practise. Cut a long green stick. Split the stick at one end for about 300mm (12in). Bind the stick at the top of the split. Push a twig down into the split to hold it open.

Fish are best speared at night. Crouch on the river bank. Hold the head of a small flashlight in the water, spear ready in the other hand. The light will attract fish. Plunge the spear down. The holding twig will be pushed away by the fish's body and the split stick will snap, holding the fish fast.

Fishing with a line

Fishing with hook and line takes a lot of patience but is worth trying if you have a lot of time to pass. Anything will make the hook — a pin, a thorny twig, a sharply pointed piece of wood. Bait could be worms or caterpillars, grubs etc. The line could be made of twine, electric plastic-covered electric wire or even thin strips of rag.

Preserving fish

If you managed to catch two or three fish, you would cook one for your supper right away. But you might not catch fish the next day and, in a survival camp, it is a good idea to make food last as long as possible when you can get hold of it. American Red Indians used to hang strips of buffalo meat to dry in the sun and wind. When fresh buffalo meat was hard to get, they always had something to eat.

You can preserve fish by smoking. Meat can be smoked too but it takes a very long time — up to 12 hours. All you need for smoking fish is a smoking box, made from two tin boxes with lids, and some sawdust or wood chips.

Prepare the fish first
Slit the underbelly of the fish. Cut the head off. Clean out the insides. Wash the fish.

Making the smoke box
Pierce holes all over the bottom of one tin box. Sprinkle a layer of sawdust or wood chips over the bottom of the second tin box. The sawdust or chips must be from oak or ash trees. Oak makes the best flavour. Pine trees chips are not good to use. The resin gets on the food.

Make a small fire in the sawdust or wood chips and then, when it is going well, heap more dust or chips on top. It should be about 25mm (1in) deep all over. The wood will start to smoulder and smoke. Lay the fish inside the pierced tin. Rest the tin on top of the smoking box. Put the lid on. The smoke rises through the pierced holes and smokes the fish. This is called 'curing'. The fish will be smoked in about 2—3 hours. Eat smoked fish hot or cold. It does not need any further cooking. You can also smoke sausages in a smoke box. They will need frying afterwards but it makes them taste different and very delicious!

Reef knot

Knots

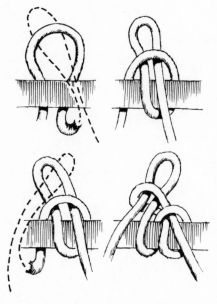

Highwayman's hitch

Clove hitch

Round turn and two half-hitches

Knots are useful in all kinds of ways. Some are used to hold parcels and bundles together. Others are used for lifting weights or for pulling things along. Some knots are tied on the end of ropes to stop things sliding off the end. There are dozens of uses for knots in camping and besides knots, you need to know about lashing cords. Lashings are used to hold pieces of wood together.

Some useful knots and lashings are illustrated. Practise them with a length of rope or cord — not string — until you can tie them in the dark. One day you may have to!

Reef knot This is a safe knot and is used for fastening two ends of rope together.

Highwayman's hitch This is said to be the knot used by highwaymen to tie up a horse outside an inn so that they could make a quick get-away. Watch cowboys the next time you see a western film. They use the same hitch to tie up their horses outside the saloon! You can use it for tying a line to a fence when you might want to pull it free quickly.

Clove hitch This is the knot to use when there is a downwards pull. You have to learn to tie a clove hitch before you can practise square lashing (see page 104).

Round turn and two half-hitches This is a knot you use when you want to put up a line between two trees such as for drying clothes or making a temporary shelter with a ground sheet. This knot is used when there is pull from one side.

Sheet bend This is a knot used a lot by yachtsmen and sailors. It is used for joining ropes or cords of different thicknesses so that they do not pull apart.

Timber hitch This is a useful knot if you have to pull something heavy along on a rope — such as a log for the camp fire. It is important to be able to do it because it is also the beginning of diagonal lashing (see page 105).

Marline spike hitch This is a knot used often in sailing. You can use it to make a ladder or perhaps a hanger for clothes.

Miller's knot This useful knot closes the neck of bags very securely. It was probably used by millers to tie the necks of flour bags. Sailors sometimes use it for tying the necks of their kit bags.

Bowline This is one of the most important knots you can learn. It is used a great deal in rescue work. The knot makes a loop in the rope which cannot slip.

Timber hitch

Marline spike hitch

Sheet bend

Bowline

Miller's knot

Climbing and rescue kno

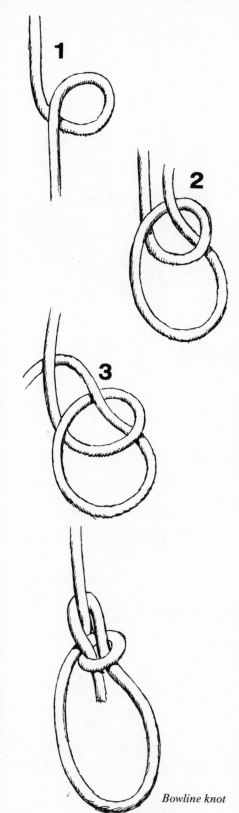

Climbing is a sport all on its own and should be taken seriously. You will probably have to do a little hill climbing on your walks and treks, but real mountain climbing has to be learned. Adventuring in the long holidays may give you a taste for climbing. If it does, the best thing you can do is to join one of the young people's outdoor organisations. You will find some more information about these on page 141.

It is useful to know one or two climbing knots because sometimes they are used in rescue. Practise these climbing knots with a piece of plastic clothes line. This feels rather like a real nylon climbing rope. **But a word of warning that you must always remember: never use a clothes line as a climbing rope even for fun.** It is not strong enough and will break. You can only use a clothes line for practising knots.

Bowline knot

If you were stranded on a mountain ledge and a rope was passed down to you by the rescue team, you would tie yourself to the rope with a bowline. Practise tying this knot round your waist so that you will always know how to do it properly in an emergency.

Double-knotted bowline. When you can knot a bowline, go on and learn how to tie a double-knotted bowline. This is even safer than the ordinary bowline because once knotted it cannot work loose.

Figure-of-eight

If you were learning to climb properly, you would be taught how to anchor yourself to the mountain face. This is called 'belaying'. There are different ways of belaying, but the simplest is a loop of rope

Bowline knot

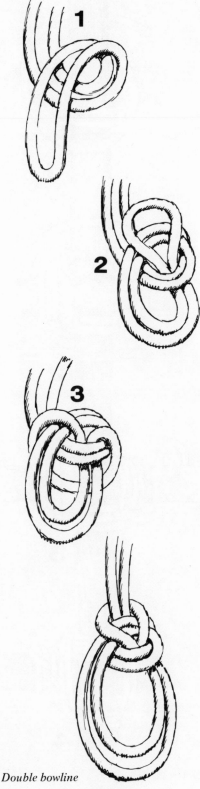

tied with a figure-of-eight knot. The figure-of-eight knot is also used by climbers to attach the safety rope to their waistbelts. Practise tying a figure-of-eight knot over a post.

Figure-of-eight knot
1   Double the rope to make a loop.
2   Fold the loop down and then pass it round the doubled rope.
3   Take the loop through the new doubled-rope loop and pull tightly.

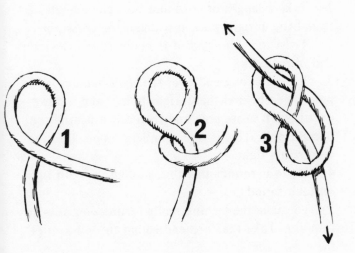

Figure-of-eight

Double bowline

Lashings

Look at the illustration of camp furniture on page 107. You can see that to join wooden poles together they are sometimes set square over each other, and sometimes diagonally. The cord lashings used to hold the joins have to be very tight and secure. Otherwise the furniture falls apart as soon as it is used. When you can lash properly, you can make all kinds of gadgets. Use strong cord rather than rope for lashing.

Square lashing

Lay one pole across another. In these instructions, the pole underneath is called the upright pole. The pole lying across is called the cross pole.

1   Take a length of cord and tie a clove hitch round the upright pole, just under the cross pole.

2   Twist the short end of the cord round the long end of the cord.

3   Take the long end over the right hand cross pole. Then behind the upright pole. Take it down over the left cross pole and then down behind the upright pole. This is one complete round. Pull the cord really tight.

4   Do four rounds like this, pulling the cord tight on each round.

5   To make the lashing really secure, you now do frapping. Take the cord end round the left arm of the cross pole.

6   Wind the cord round and round the upright pole about three times.

7   Finish off with a clove hitch on the right arm of the cross pole.

Square lashing

Diagonal lashing

Lay one pole over another diagonally. For these instructions, call the pole underneath the under pole. Call the pole lying on top the top pole.

1 Start by making a timber hitch where the two poles cross.

2 Wind the cord round the two poles so that the turns lie over the timber hitch. Make three turns. Pull each turn tight.

3 Now make three turns round the crossed poles the other way. Pull each turn tightly.

4 Make three frapping turns round the top pole. Pull each frapping turn tightly.

5 Finish with a clove hitch.

Diagonal lashing

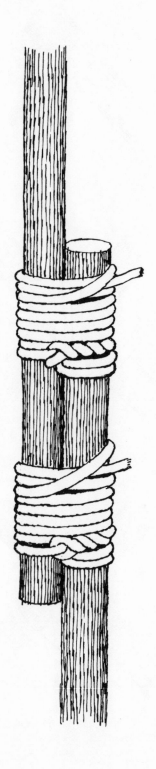

Sheer lashing

Sheer lashing is not often used in making camp furniture but you would find it useful if you wanted to join two poles together to make a long length.

1 Lay the two poles side by side, the ends overlapping. Two sheer lashings are used to hold the poles together.

2 Make a timber hitch to hold the two poles together. Wind the cord round the poles about eight times.

3 Finish with a clove hitch.

4 Make the second lashing in the same way.

5 To prevent the lashings from slipping, hammer small pieces of wood between the two poles. This holds the poles firmly against the cords and makes the lashings more secure.

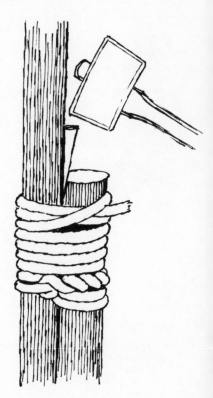

Sheer lashing

Camp furniture

You already know how to make a crane and a
cooking pot for the camp fire. (Page 85). There are
several pieces of camp furniture that you can make
if you are going to be around the camp for some
time. Camp furniture is not absolutely necessary but
it is fun to be able to spend your time in camp
usefully. Do not cut wood from a living bush or
tree. You can always find green pieces of wood
lying on the ground.

Plate rack
This is the easiest of all. Lay two fairly thick
branches side by side on the ground. Push thin
sticks into the ground along each side of the
branches. Stand the clean plates between the sticks.

Cup rack
A branch with some twigs on it will make a cup
rack. Sharpen one end of the branch and push it
into the ground so that it stands firmly. Hang the
cups on the twigs.

Wash stand
Tie three thick poles together with a diagonal
lashing. (See page 105 for a diagonal lashing). Stand
a bowl on top.

Hanging larder
This is just the thing for keeping flies away from
fresh meat or fish. You need a piece of muslin or
thin cotton fabric. Fold it in half overlapping the
long sides. Tie the bottom together with a Miller's
knot (see page 101) to make a bag. Put a large plate
inside the bag. Tie a piece of twine to the handle of
a saucepan lid. Put the lid inside the bag. Fasten the
top of the bag with a Miller's knot. Hang the bag
from a branch by the line tied to the saucepan lid.

*A wash stand is a useful piece of
camp furniture you can make with
sticks and cord*

Tree climber
Tie loops in a long length of rope. One person climbs up a lookout tree and secures the rope end. Everyone can use the tree climber by putting their feet in the loops.

Lights and lamps
It is a good idea to have a flashlight with you in camp so that you can find your way about if you have to get up in the night. Put it in your shoe so that you can easily find it in the dark. For general camp lighting you will probably use a candle in a holder of some kind.

Making a candlestick
A flat stone can be used for a simple candlestick or the candle can be stood in an empty glass jar. Light the candle first and hold it over the empty jar so that some melted wax drips onto the bottom. Immediately stand the candle in the melted wax. This is a good candle-holder for a windy night. The jar shields the candle from the wind.

Penknife holder
Ram one blade of a penknife into a tree or pole. Open the blade at the other end half way so that it stands up. Push a candle onto the blade.

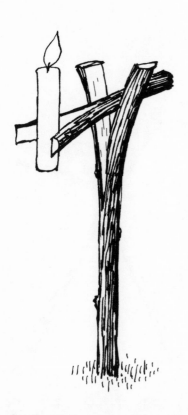

Tin can holder
Pierce a hole in the side of a shallow tin can. With a pair of metal cutters, cut a cross on the pierced hole. Bend the points of the cross inwards. Push a candle through the hole.

Wood holders
Look for a green stick, about 37mm (1½in) diameter. Split one end for about 150mm (6in) push a thin

Candlestick from a pierced can and another to make from split pieces of wood

stick down into the split to hold it apart. Push in
the candle and pull out the stick.

Two pieces of wood will make a bracket candle
holder. Look at the illustration. Or a piece of strong
twine can be used instead of a second stick. Prepare
the candle holder by splitting the end. Open the
split and push in a looped piece of twine. Pull out
the wedge. Put a candle in the loop and pull the
ends tight to hold the candle securely.

Making candles

You will always plan to take enough candles with
you on a camping trip, even if you are trekking into
the wilds. But supposing you had to make a candle.
Could you do it? Your ancestors made their own
candles from animal fat.

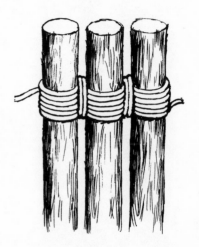

This is how they did it. It is always useful to
know how things used to be made before machines
made them.

Sheep fat, with a little pig fat, was boiled with
water. The fat melted and rose to the top. It was
skimmed off and boiled up again. Candle makers
did this at least twice. The thick tallow which was
made from the fat was yellow in colour. Cotton or
linen thread made the candle wick. The threads
were twisted between the fingers, then doubled and
twisted again, to make a thick wick. The wick was
tied to a stick, dipped in melted tallow and left
hanging to harden off. Every time the tallow
hardened, the wick was dipped in melted tallow
again. At every dipping the candle got a bit thicker.
Nowadays most candles are made in moulds from
paraffin wax although some candle makers still
make candles in the old way, using beeswax instead
of tallow.

*Tripod lashing: you can make all
kinds of furniture with this*

Let's go for a swim

Let's go for a swim!
If you are camping with friends and there is some water nearby, someone is going to suggest swimming. Those who cannot swim will not be tempted to try. Good swimmers will be keen to get into the water, especially if it is a hot day. Just the same, even if you can swim some things need thinking about before you plunge in!

On the sea shore
A gradual slope of sand is safe enough for swimming but not when the tide is turning. Steep slopes, especially those with rocks on them, can graze the knees. Rough seas are never safe enough to swim in. The noise of the waves alone would make it hard to hear anyone who was in trouble.

Keep a lookout for lifeguard's warnings which are put up on some beaches — and obey them! Ask people who seem to know the beach about tides and currents.

Rivers
You have to be very careful of river currents, particularly if there is a weir or waterfall downstream. Rivers are usually colder than the sea so be prepared for a cold shock! If the water is shallow enough for a swimmer to stand up, someone should check the river bottom. There may be broken glass on it, or sharp tins. It is worth keeping plimsoles or sandshoes on to protect your feet from possible cuts. Keep away from reeds and weedy places.

Lakes and ponds
The bottom of lakes and ponds can be very soft mud which is as dangerous as quicksand. Test it

first. There may also be rocks and branches lying on the bottom. Make sure that there is a place where you can get out of the water easily. Watch for underground springs flowing into lakes. They can be icy cold and can give a swimmer cramp.

Water-sense
Every year, thousands of people get drowned. Some get drowned because they get into difficulties with a boat. Most of them get drowned because they cannot swim. There are no excuses for anyone not being able to swim. You may feel that you do not like water very much and that you do not enjoy swimming. But you must learn to do it. If you cannot swim and you get into difficulties in a boat or fall into water, you stand a very good chance of losing your life.

Survival methods
Even when you can swim properly, there may be times when you need to know how to stay afloat until help comes. Practise floating and drown proofing in a swimming pool.

Floating
Lay back on the water so that you are looking at the ceiling or the sky. Your ears will be under water. Let your legs come up naturally. Stretch your arms out in the water just above your shoulder level. You should be able to float like this for quite a long time.

Next, try sculling with your hands. Bring your arms down to your sides but away from your body. Close your fingers and curve your hands. By paddling your hands slowly back and forwards you will be able to move along in the water, still floating on your back.

*Drown-proofing helps
you to stay afloat even in rough sea*

Drown proofing

If you were in a rough sea, floating or treading water would not be easy to do. Drown-proofing would help you to stay afloat. It does not take as much effort as treading water and you would not get tired as quickly. Practise first at home in the wash basin. Fill the basin with water and then put your face into the water.

Open your eyes. Do not hold your breath with an effort. Simply 'close your nose' at the back. Do this as though you were breathing out — but do not actually let any air out. Then, gently let the air out of your lungs through your mouth. To breathe, turn your head sideways out of the water, breathe in and then look down again. Practise this until you can breathe out and breathe in again slowly and without panicking. Then try it in a swimming pool.

Get into the water and take a deep breath. Fall gently forward into the water, your arms held loosely. Keep your mouth shut and your eyes open. Your upper body will level out in the water, your legs will hang loosely. When you want to breathe in, press down gently with your arms. Lift your head sideways out of the water. Do not lift suddenly. Keep all your movements slow.

Using a life-belt

It is surprising how few people would know what to do if a lifebelt were thrown to them. The idea is that you get it round your body as quickly as possible. Here is what you should do. Grab hold of the lifebelt with your hands on top of it. Push it down into the water as though you were trying to lift yourself on to it. The far side of the lifebelt will come up. Now push the side you are holding onto away from you under the water. The side that is in the air will fall forward onto you. Push

Life saving

yourself through the hole and get your elbows onto the lifebelt.

Life saving
One day, you might see someone in difficulties and drowning. If you are in the water and near to them, and you know how to do life-saving, you can help immediately. If you are on the shore, diving in and swimming out may not be the best thing to do.

Look around and see if anyone else is swimming who may not have noticed the emergency. Shout and point to show where the victim is. Look to see if there is an adult nearby. Make sure that they understand what is happening. If there is no one else and everything depends on you, and you are a very strong swimmer, you will have to get to the person who is in trouble. If there is a lifeline with a lifebelt, get it and see if you can wade out far enough to throw it. If the victim is too far out, you will have to swim to them to give help. Take off your shoes, jacket, and trousers or skirt before getting into the water. Act quickly but use commonsense!

Rescue
Having reached the person who is drowning, your real problems begin. They will grab at you and you can both be pulled under water. You have to try and calm and relax them. Get behind and turn the victim onto his back. Put an arm over his shoulder, across his chest and place your hand on his ribs. In this position, the victim's legs will float and you can begin to make your way to the shore towing him behind you.

Kiss of life

Everyone ought to know how to do the Kiss of Life. If you can start someone breathing again, you may save their life.

Lay the victim flat on the ground with his head tilted backwards. Make sure that there is nothing in his mouth. Put your mouth over the victim's mouth and breathe air into him. If for any reason you cannot breathe air into the mouth, put your mouth over the victim's nose. Make the first four breaths quickly and then about 4 seconds apart. If you hear gurgling noises coming from the victim's chest he has water in him. Turn him onto his shoulder and push his head down lower than his chest so that the water comes out.

Keep breathing air into the unconscious victim until help comes or he comes round.

If you can, get someone to practise this with you. It is harder to do than it sounds.

Tracking

Wild creatures live all around us, but some people never notice them. Even in towns and cities there are small animals in the parks and open spaces. Many wild birds make their homes as happily among the tall buildings as they do in the countryside.

We may not always see the wild creatures but they leave signs behind. Signs like footprints, tracks, droppings and the remains of meals. Native hunters in the bush and in the jungle look for these signs. They can not only tell exactly what kind of animal made the track but how fast it was moving and how recently it passed that way.

Being a 'nature detective' and learning how to read the signs is a fascinating hobby. It makes trekking so much more interesting.

Where to find tracks

Footprints and trails are easiest to see in fresh snow. But if the sun is shining, tracks can begin to thaw round the sides quite quickly. This can sometimes fool you into thinking that a much bigger animal has made the footprints. Muddy ground takes tracks well. Look in the mud around the edges of ditches, ponds and streams for signs of animals and birds coming to drink. The beach at low tide is another good place to do your detecting. Try sand dunes too, in the early morning before the dew has dried.

After rain, when the earth is damp, tracks can be seen on footpaths and in places without much grass. Sometimes, bird tracks can be found in the thin mud left after a puddle has dried up.

When a hare runs, its back legs come forward in front of the fore feet

Pawed animals have five clawed toes and a pad under the foot

Deer, goats, pigs and sheep have a cloven hoof

Horses, ponies and donkeys have only one 'toe' and make a round hoof mark

Compare the sizes of a big wolf's feet with those of a dog!

Whose footprint?

To be able to identify which animal made the footprint, you have to know a bit about animal feet. There are two main types of animal feet, hoofs and paws. Hoof marks are made by animals such as horses and ponies, donkeys and mules, deer, goats, sheep and pigs. There are two kinds of hoof marks. Horses, ponies, donkeys and mules have only one 'toe' and this makes a round hoof mark. Deer, goats, sheep and pigs have four 'toes' but only the middle two are like hoofs and make footprints. This kind of animal is described as having split or 'cloven' hoofs.

Animals with paws have five clawed toes on each foot. Sometimes the shortest toe, on the inside of the foot (where you have your big toe), does not make a track mark because it is too short. All five of a badger's toes show in his footprint because he puts his feet down flat as he walks. Bears walk in the same way. So do hedgehogs.

Pawed animals have a pad under the foot and this also makes a mark. Sometimes, the animal's claws make marks. Squirrel tracks and tracks made by moles, shrews, mice and rats show claws quite clearly. Beaver footprints show claws and so do those of the wild cats such as pine martens, polecats and wolverines. Domestic cats pull in their claws as they walk, and so do lynxes.

A dog footprint shows four toes, the pads underneath, and also the claw marks. You can usually tell the size of the dog from the size of the prints. Compare the footprint made by a big dog with the footprint of a wolf!

Rabbits and hares have hairy feet with hair between the toes so the pad marks do not show. But you can recognise footprints made by these animals easily.

Footprint patterns

The way an animal puts its feet down as it walks or runs helps a nature detective to find out who made the footprints. Hares and rabbits hop or leap across the ground. The front feet go down first and then the back legs come forward in front of the forefeet. The animal kicks the back legs straight behind and goes into a leap or hop. He lands on his front feet and then the back legs come forward again. This movement means that in a group of four paw marks, the two short marks at the back are made by the smaller front feet. The two longer paw marks at the front, almost in line, are made by the back feet. Squirrels move by hopping and their tracks lie close together in groups of four. Animals with long tails, such as musk rats and coypus, leave a line behind their footprints made by the dragging tail.

The tracks made by an animal walking look different from those made when it is running or galloping. Look at the picture of tracks made by a deer walking and then the same deer running. When it walks, the deer puts its back feet almost on the same marks made by the front feet. When the deer starts to trot, the space between the hoof marks widens. At a gallop, the marks are quite wide apart.

Now you can see how a hunter stalks his prey. When he sees fresh footprints of an animal walking, he can, if he is very careful and quiet, creep up behind it before the animal has a chance to start running away.

Front feet and back feet
In some animals, the front or fore feet and the back or hind feet are more or less the same size. In others, the fore and hind feet are different sizes. Squirrels, voles and shrews, have large hind feet. So do beavers. A brown bear has a wide front foot and a narrower hind foot.

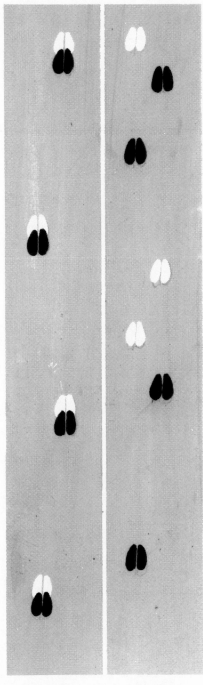

Walking   *Running*

When a deer walks, it puts its back feet almost on the same mark made by the front feet but look how the footprints change when the deer starts to run!

Bird signs and tracks

You have to be quite an expert to be able to tell what kind of bird made the tracks you are studying because all birds have four toes, three pointing forward and one pointing backwards. Swimming birds have webs between their toes, so you can easily identify ducks, swans and gull footprints. But an observant nature detective can find out something about what the bird was doing from other signs.

Feeding birds
A big stone with fairly large bird footprints round it and a few broken snail shells tells you that a thrush has been feeding. You know that it is a thrush's feeding place because blackbirds have never learned the trick of banging a shell open to get at the snail! Woodpeckers are clever in the way they break open nutshells. They wedge the nut into a crack to hold it secure while they peck away. If you find a pile of broken shells at the foot of a tree or post look up and you may see nutshells still rammed into cracks. Some small birds peck away at nuts while they are still growing on the tree. If you find fruit stones neatly broken into two, you will know that the hawfinch with its big, strong beak has been feeding.

Pellets
Sometimes, at the foot of a tree or a post, you will find small, strange-looking lumps on the ground. They appear to be made up of pieces of bone or seeds, sometimes mixed up with fur scraps or feathers. These are pellets. Most birds spit out two every day. Pellets are the parts of a bird's food that it cannot digest. It is quite natural for a bird to get rid of it. If you look at a pellet closely you might be able to tell what kind of bird spat it out. A pellet from a bird of prey would have fur, feathers and

Stalking animals

bits of bone on it. A sea bird pellet might have
pieces of shell and fish bones all mixed up together.

Stalking animals
Stalking is the word used by hunters when they are
creeping up on their prey. It need not mean
harming or killing an animal. It can be a way of
getting close to a creature so that you can study it
without the animal knowing you are there.

Stalking is best done alone because one stalker
moving in the right way is likely to get closer and
unseen than two. Many animals not only have a
keen sense of smell (they will smell you long before
you can even see them) they also have very good
eyesight or hearing. Some even pick up vibrations
of movement in the ground or from bushes or trees.
Slow, careful movements are very important if you
are going to get close enough to watch.

Study their habits first
It helps to know something of the way an animal
lives before you set out to stalk it. Find out where
the animal makes its home. What senses does it use
to spot danger? What does it eat, and at what time
of day? You can get this kind of information from
nature books.

The den or lair can sometimes be discovered by
following the trail an animal leaves as it moves
about through the woods and fields. Once you have
recognised its den, move away so that you are out
of sight. Wait for the animal to return.

The best time to spot animals near their homes
is early in the morning or, of they are night movers,
just before dusk.

Dens, lairs and setts
A fox's den (called his 'earth') is easy to recognise.

Foxes usually make their dens on a warm, south-facing slope in sandy or gravelly soil. The entrance hole is fairly small, about 200 — 250mm (8—10in) across. The soil the fox has dug out is spread in a fan-shaped heap outside. If you want to find out if the fox earth is being used by a fox or not, just stick your head near the hole and sniff. Foxes have a strong, sharp-smelling 'animal' smell. Your nose will soon tell you if the den has been used recently!

A badger's home is called a 'sett'. Badgers choose the same kind of place as foxes but they are a bit tidier about their digging. Badgers move the soil they have dug out a short distance away from the entrance hole, leaving a kind of furrow in front. Also, badgers line their holes with soft pieces of moss and dried leaves and sometimes you can find pieces outside the sett.

Rabbit warrens are easy to find in woods and fields but a hare's form is more difficult to spot. Hares do not make a proper nest or burrow, they simply scratch out a shallow place to lie in and this is called the 'form'. The back end of the form is wider and deeper than the front end. You can find forms tucked up against a rock or a clump of grass so that the hare is sheltered from the wind. Hares sleep in forms even in the winter, digging a place in the snow.

Deer also live without a proper home. They simply lie down to sleep in a sheltered place. You can usually see where they have been sleeping because the plants and grasses have been flattened out.

How to stalk

When you are stalking, wear brown, grey or green-coloured clothing, so that you blend in with the background. Most animals are said to be colour blind, but they will certainly spot a white shirt more easily than they will a grey one! Soldiers wear camouflaged clothing splotched with green and brown when they do not want to be seen and you might try making yourself a special stalking outfit by painting an old shirt or jacket with fabric paints.

When you think you have discovered the home den, check which way the wind is blowing first. If the wind is blowing from behind you towards the animal, he will be able to smell you. Also, the wind will carry any sounds you make towards him. Approach with the wind coming from the animal's direction towards you.

Use your eyes and ears and move very carefully and very slowly. Do not make any sudden movements. If you think the animal has heard you, freeze instantly and wait until it is reassured. Among trees, you might be able to walk upright, taking advantage of trunks and bushes for cover. Look where you are placing your feet. Do not step onto dried sticks that will snap, or rustle through leaves. As soon as you are close enough to see the animal, stop. Do not move again until the animal has gone.

In open country, you must crawl on your stomach, moving forward on your elbows and hands, pushing your feet behind you. As soon as you get close enough to see the animal, drop your head, lie quite flat and watch without moving.

Plaster casts

If your hobby is stalking and watching animals you cannot very well take one home with you for a specimen! Even if you caught a small animal, it would probably die in captivity because you could not feed it properly. Anyway, it is cruel to take a creature away from its surroundings. Sometimes you will find bones and skulls of animals and you can take these home. Or you can take photographs of lairs and dens for study collection.

You can also take plaster casts of animal's footprints and these make very good specimens for a nature collection. You need some plaster of Paris powder. This can be bought from builder's merchants, and some do-it-yourself shops. Chemists and druggists sometimes sell it as 'dental plaster'. Plaster of Paris is not very expensive and you do not need a great deal of it. A footprint will take only 100gr. (4oz) of powder.

You also need something to carry water in, a tin can to mix the plaster in, a spoon and some salt in a small box. Carry your plaster powder in a tin box with a lid.

How it is done
When you find a suitable footprint lift anything out of it that could spoil the print — stones, twigs or large pieces of soil. If the track is on sloping ground, you might have to build up a 'wall' on the shallow side so that the plaster does not run out of the print. Pour a little water into the tin mug and gradually spoon in the plaster powder, stirring it. When the mixture feels like thick cream, add a pinch of salt. This helps the plaster to set more quickly. Pour the plaster into the footprint filling the hole right to the top. The plaster should be at least 15mm (¾in) thick otherwise the cast will break when you lift it out. Now wait for the plaster to

dry. If the ground is damp, or if it is a wet day, drying could take about 20 minutes.

Making a hanger

If you want to hang your casting, the hanger must be put into the plaster before it dries. A piece of string makes a good hanger. Cut a piece about 100m (4in) long. Knot the ends. Push the knot into the wet plaster at the edge of the footprint, with the loop lying on the ground. As the plaster dries, the string is firmly fixed into the casting.

When the cast is dry

Work the soil loose all round. Lift the casting out of the ground very carefully. Some soil will be sticking to the casting. Leave it for the moment. Take the casting home and put it somewhere warm to dry out overnight. The next day, wash off the soil. Scrape the back of the casting with a knife blade to level it. Write on the name of the animal and where you found the footprint. Hang up the casting by the string loop.

How to be a plant hunter

Being a plant hunter can be as exciting a hobby as stalking and watching wildlife. There are so many different wild plants to be found everywhere — in the countryside, in forests and woods, on mountainsides, on the sea shore — even in the cities and towns. Once you start to hunt for the different kinds, you will soon become interested in keeping a record of your plant-hunting expeditions in a diary. Studying plants is called 'botany' and plant hunters are called 'botanists'.

What you need
To be able to identify plants you need a botanical encyclopedia. This is a kind of illustrated dictionary with pictures of all the plants there are and lists of their names. You do not need to buy an encyclopedia. Most libraries have copies and you can easily borrow one when you need it. A notebook with both plain and lined pages is useful for keeping a record of your finds.

The most important thing a plant hunter needs is something in which to carry home specimens. Botanists have a tin box on a carrying strap called a 'vasculum'. If you can find a fairly large, flat, tin box with a lid, this will do just as well. You will also have to have something with which to cut plants. A razor blade in a safety holder is best. Or a small pair of very sharp scissors.

Making a start
Line the tin box with a piece of damp blotting paper before you begin. When you find a plant you want, cut just a single stem. It should have a flower, a fully grown leaf, a bud if possible. If it is the right time of year, cut a stem with a seed pod or fruit.

Never tug at the plant. Never pull the whole plant out by its roots. If you should find a plant which you think might be rare and it has only one flower on it, leave the plant alone. If the flower is taken, the plant cannot seed. Without seeds, there will be no new plants and that kind of plant may disappear completely.

Getting your plants home
You have a good day in the country and you have three or four good specimens that you do not recognise. Now begins the detective work. Put the plants in fresh water and study them. Look at the shape of the leaves and flower petals. Count the petals. You will probably have to spend a long time poring over the encyclopedia before you find your particular plant. When you do find it you will see that plants have two names. One is easy to read and is its common name. The second name is in Latin. This is the plant's botanical name. The botanical name is important because that is the name by which the plant is known all over the world. Sometimes, another word appears after the botanical name. This is the name of the botanist who either discovered the plant or named it. Supposing you found a yellow Horned Poppy on a shingly beach. You would quickly discover that its botanical name was *Glaucium flavum* and the word 'Crantz' is given afterwards. Another search and you would find out that a botanist called Heinrich von Crantz who lived in Vienna in the 18th century named your pretty yellow flower.

Keeping a record
Now you know quite a lot about your plant specimen and you can start your botany record. Note where you found the plant, the date and anything else which seems interesting to you. Write in the plant's two names. Add the botanist's name

and anything else which you can find out about
him. If you can draw, you might do a watercolour
sketch of the plant before it wilts. Or you can try
another interesting hobby — preserving flowers and
plants by drying and pressing them.

Preserving flowers and plants
Flowers, leaves, grasses and seed heads are
preserved in different ways, depending on what you
want to use them for. Flowers and leaves can be
dried by pressing them flat. This is the best way to
keep flowers in a nature diary. Glue the pressed
flowers to the page with a touch of clear glue. Seed
heads, grasses and some flowers and leaves will dry
out attractively if they are simply left on the plant
in autumn. These are the plants you should collect
if you want to make flower arrangements.

Pressing flowers
Pressing flowers is a lovely hobby for both boys and
girls. Collect and press your flowers in summer and
during the winter months you can arrange your
collection in a nature diary. Real flower presses can
be bought in some toy shops and craft shops but
you can press flowers in a big book just as well. The
book should be thick and have large-sized pages.
You also need some sheets of white blotting paper
or a box of white handkerchief tissues. Open the
book near the back. Lay a sheet of blotting paper
on the page (or three sheets of handkerchief tissue).
Arrange some flowers on the paper. They should
not touch. (If the flowers have thick centres, slice
them in half with a razor blade in a safety holder.)
Put another sheet of blotting paper (or three more
sheets of tissue) on top of the flowers. Close about
twenty pages of the book over the flowers. Lay
another sheet of blotting paper on the page and do

*Hang plants to dry in a cool,
dark place, heads down*

the same again. Go on until the book is full — but not so full that it will not close. Put the book away somewhere with a weight on top. A kitchen weight will do. Do not touch the book for at least three weeks. This is very important. Anyone can press flowers if they have patience and do not keep looking to see how everything is getting on. After three weeks, open the book carefully. (Try not to puff and blow or the dry, papery flowers will fly about!) Lift the dried flowers carefully with tweezers and put them between sheets of clean paper until you are ready to use them.

Sprays of leaves and bracken can be dried under the carpet and arranged on sheets of newspaper.

Standing and hanging plants

To dry seed heads, bracken and grasses, pick them on a dry day and tie six stems together tightly. Or use a small rubber band. Fix up a line in a cool, dark place, such as a garage or an outhouse. Sometimes a loft will do if there is not too much light. Tie the bunches to the line and leave them to dry. This can take as much as a month. Seed heads and grasses will also dry when standing in an empty jar or can. Leave the jar in a dark room. Too much light will make the colours fade.

Making 'immortelles'

Arrangements made of dried plants are called 'immortelles'. They make lovely decorations for party tables. Look for a fallen tree branch that has some bark left on it. Break off a piece and take it home. Push some modelling clay onto the bark. Use dark green or brown clay if you can. Break the stems of dried seed heads and grasses to about 100mm (4in) long. Push the stems into the clay.

Some plants, grasses and seed heads will dry if left standing in a jar

Glue nuts, fir cones, acorns and dried leaves round the base. You can leave the arrangement in its natural colours and spray it with clear varnish, or paint it with gold or silver paint. Making 'immortelles' is a good way of using the beautiful and interesting things than can be found on nature walks.

Pressing leaves

Even if you live in a town you can still find leaves to press. Parks are full of trees and, on a windy day in autumn the paths will be covered with fallen leaves in beautiful colours — red, gold, bronze and yellow. Collect the prettiest and take them home. Iron the leaves with a warm iron to dry them completely. Dried leaves can be used to make greetings cards. Glue them to a piece of folded card.

Display boards

Some things display better if they are glued to a board. You might make a arrangement showing the growth cycle of a plant for instance, picking first the shoot, then the plant with its buds, followed by the flowers. Finish with the seed or fruit. Write in the date on which you picked each specimen.

Bird pellets make interesting displays too. If you found several pellets, it would be interesting to take one to pieces and display the contents beside a complete pellet. A drawing or photograph of the bird and some information about its size, nest and eggs, would make a very worthwhile exhibit for your museum.

Making clay pots

Making clay pots

Primitive people made their camps near to rivers and streams, not just so that they could get water but also so that they could find clay for making their cooking pots. There may be clay in the ground near your home. Look for it on the banks of streams and in the meadows along the sides of the river.

When you dig clay out of the ground it is in sticky lumps — yellowish-brown, grey, red or blue-grey. It will have bits of dead leaves in it, twigs, stones and soil. Before you can use the clay, it must be cleaned. You can do this in one of two ways. If you have a lot of time to spare let the clay dry out hard and then break it up into small pieces. Pick out the biggest lumps of rubbish. Put the bits of clay into a bucket and pour on a little water.

If you want to get going more quickly, put the dirty clay into a bucket and pour water on it. Swish the lump around until the clay dissolves. Pour the thick clay and water mixture through a garden sieve so that the bits of rubbish are trapped. Force the clay through the sieve with an old stiff brush.

Leave the thick clay to settle for two or three days and then pour off the top water. The clay now has to be dried. Plop the clay onto a wooden or concrete surface and leave it to dry a little.

Depending on which method you used to clean the clay, you have now got to the same stage. The clay you dried out will have soaked up enough water in the bucket. Squeeze it into a lump. The clay you washed with water will have dried out enough to handle. Now the clay has to be kneaded to make it smooth and plastic.

Kneading clay

Put the clay on the table and push the lump flat with the heel of your hands. (The heel is just above the wrist.) Pick up the sides of the lump with your finger tips and then push with the heels of your hands again. Roll the clay out, thump it about. Keep doing this until it feels smooth and does not break when you roll it out. Keep clay in a plastic bag to stop it drying out.

Coil pots

One of the ways in which potters make pots is by coiling. You can make a small pot in the same way. Your pot will dry hard if you leave it in the sun but it will not hold liquid because it won't have been baked and glazed in a kiln. Glazing puts a glassy surface on pottery.

The clay should be fairly damp for coiling. It if has got a bit too dry and stiff, knead it again on a wetted surface. Break off a bit of clay that just fits into your palm. Squeeze it to make a cigar shape.

Roll the clay out on a flat surface using both hands. Make a long, even coil. The coil should not have bumps in it. It should be the same thickness all the way along. Make several coils and put them on one side covered with a damp cloth. Take another piece of clay and roll it into a ball. Flatten the ball to make a disc. Wet the surface of the disc. Pick up the first coil and lay it round the edge of the disc. Press it down so that it sticks. Wind the coil round and round, dampening it as you go to make the clay stick to itself. Put your fingers inside the pot and smear the edges of the coils together. You can smear the outside of the pot as well if you like or just leave the coils as they are. Keep adding new coils, overlapping and smearing the ends together until your pot is as tall as you like. Leave it to dry

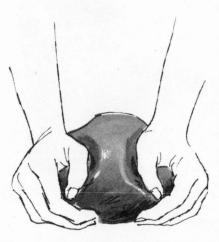

in the sun. You can 'bake' your pot in a fire pit kiln
if you have some garden peat or sawdust handy.

Fire-pit kiln

Lift a patch of grass off the ground with a spade
(see page 66). Dig a hole and make a small
wood fire in the bottom. When the fire is going
well, put a layer of dry sawdust or peat on top. Fill
your pot with sawdust or peat and put it into the
hole. Pour more sawdust or peat round the pot. If
you are firing several pots they should not touch
each other. Pour sawdust or peat between them.
Cover the pots with a thick layer of the sawdust or
peat to fill the hole. Put the piece of grass back on
top of the 'kiln' and leave it. It should smoulder
away for several days. You will see smoke coming
out round the edges of the grass. When the fire has
stopped smoking and you are sure that it is out, dig
out the baked pot very carefully.

Making a museum collection

People who do interesting jobs which involve them in research and discovery often started by being collectors. Becoming interested in one subject and learning as much as you can about it is a fascinating hobby. It could also help you towards a more interesting job when you are older.

A geologist, for instance, who works for a big oil company and spends his time looking for new sites for oil wells, might easily have collected fossils and rocks when he was young.

An archeologist, who has an exciting time digging up ancient Egyptian burial grounds or Roman settlements, probably collected stone-age implements and spear heads.

Naturalists and zoologists, who keep a watchful eye on the ecology of the world, are usually people who collected information about butterflies, insects and animal life when they were younger.

By being out and about in the countryside, you will probably begin to be interested in collecting natural things. Start a museum and arrange your collections properly so that other people can enjoy them.

Stones, rocks and fossils

Rock samples and fossils can be displayed on shelves or on a table. Find as much out as you can about your specimen. Print the name of the specimen on a small piece of paper. Fold the paper so that it stands up.

A wooden box will make a good display shelf for specimens. Paint the inside of the box a dark colour and the outside in a bright colour. Fix the box to the wall with rings and hooks or brackets. You could divide the box into smaller areas with pieces of wood or cardboard.

Making a basket

Specimen boxes

A big, shallow box or a lid can be turned into a
speciment tray with strips of cardboard. If you can
get a piece of glass cut to fit the top, you could use
the tray for small specimens, such as insects,
butterflies or shells.

Matchboxes make very good storage units too.
Glue boxes together to make a 'chest of drawers'.
Glue a paper bead to each drawer. Label the
drawers clearly so that you know what is in each.

Bush-basket

Knowing how to make baskets for storing things in
is very useful. You can buy cane and rushes from
crafts shops of course and these make very good
baskets. But it is more fun to see if you can make
baskets in the same way that primitive people made
them, gathering natural materials from the
countryside around you.

If you live near to a river or a lake, there will
probably be rushes and reeds of different kinds.
Near to the sea shore you can sometimes find long
pieces of seaweed which, dried out, make good
weaving material. In the forests, and on wild scrub
land, there are all kinds of trees and plants which
have suitable twigs and shoots.

What to look for

You need long, bendy twigs and shoots of different
thicknesses. To see if the plant is bendy enough for
weaving, try twisting a shoot around your fist. If it
does not break, it is probably the right kind. As the
same trees and shrubs do not grow everywhere in
the world, you must decide for yourself which
plants are best. Creepers, vines, clematis, wild roses,
brambles and blackthorn are the kinds of plants

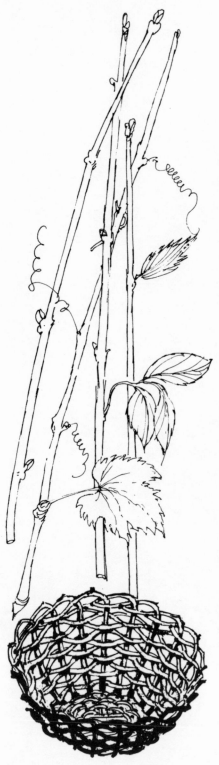

which grow long, thin stems for basket sides. Trees such as the willow, dogwood and elm grow long shoots which can be used for the basket framework. Autumn and winter, when the sap is down, are the best times for cutting twigs and shoots. Use a sharp knife and be sure to leave 50 — 100mm (2 — 4in) of budded twig for next year's regrowth.

Remember the code of the countryside: except for scrub country and wild forest, land usually belongs to someone. You should never assume that you can cut what you like. You may be ruining a cover for birds or spoiling a natural fence intended for penning animals. Think about what you are doing and ask permission first if you are in any doubt.

Weaving materials — here is what you need
Base stakes These are for the framework of the basket bottom. Cut these about the thickness of a pencil.
Base weavers These have to be fairly fine. Shoots and stems such as those of vines and creepers are about right.
Side stakes You usually need a lot of these for a basket. They should be long and of the same thickness, a little thinner than the base stakes.
Side weavers These can be almost the same thickness as the side stakes but should be a little more bendy. You need a great many.
Walers The bands at the top and bottom of the basket sides are called 'waling' and hold the basket together. Waling shoots and twigs must be long and the same thickness as the side weavers.

Getting ready to weave
Collect a lot of material before you begin. Have

more than you think you might need because some
twigs will not behave the way you want them to and
it is not worth struggling with them. Throw them
away and use others. You can weave baskets with
freshly cut material but, as the twigs dry out, the
basket will shrink a little. If you want to do the job
properly, 'fade' the twigs first. Lay the twigs and
shoots on the ground under a bush for two or three
weeks. If they should dry out too quickly, wrap the
twigs in a damp cloth for an hour or two before
using them. If shoots have thorns on them, such as
bramble or wild rose, strip the thorns by wiping the
stem firmly with a piece of thick, knitted cloth. An
old sweater is ideal.

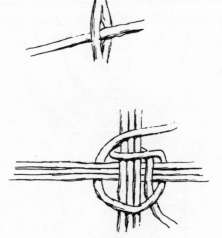

Making a basket

1　Cut a slit in the middle of three base stakes.
Push three more base stakes through the slit to
make a cross shape.
2　Take the first of the base weavers. Loop it
around the upright arm of the cross (1). Take the
left-hand end of the weaver and wind it behind arm
2 in front of arm 3 and behind arm 4. Take the
other end of the weaver in front of arm 2, behind 3
and in front of 4. Work another complete round in
the same way.

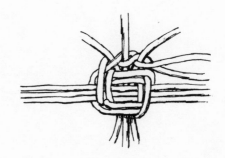

3　Now open up the arms of the cross with your
fingers so that each of the base stakes is separated.
4　Take one end of the base weaver and pass it
under the next stake. Take the other end and pass it
over the same stake. Work the first end again and
pass it over the next stake. Take the second end and
pass it under the next stake. Work round and round
like this until the base of the basket is about 125 —
150mm (5 — 6in) across. If you need to use a new
weaver, bend the new one in half and loop it
around a stake and then go on. Sharpen the end of

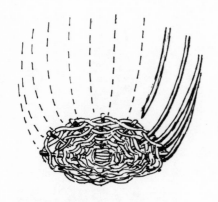

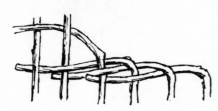

the finished weaver and push it down into the weaving.

5   When the base is finished, you are ready to start the sides. Cut 24 long side stakes. Sharpen the thicker end and push the point into the sides of the base so that the new stakes lie beside the base stakes. Push all the stakes in and then bend each one up to make the basket sides. Tie a piece of string round to hold the shape. The waling comes next.

6   In waling, three shoots are used in sequence. Start anywhere on the basket. Take waler 1 and place the end behind a stake and then take it in front of the next two stakes. Take the second waler and place it behind the next stake and weave in front of the next two. Take the third waler, place the end behind the third stake and weave it in front of the next two. Continue working each of the walers in turn, going behind a stake and in front of two. Work two complete rows.

7   The next state is called 'randing'. The weavers used for this have to be long enough to go right round the basket once with a bit left over. Use a single weaver at a time, working over a stake then under the next until the basket is as deep as you want it to be. Use new weaver shoots as you need them, pushing the end of the old one down into the weaving.

Work two more rows of waling as stage 6.

8   Bordering. There are several different ways of making the top border of a basket. This is the simplest. Leave about 20cm (8in) of the side stakes unwoven. Start anywhere. Bend stake 1 to the right, behind the stake next to it, then in front of the next and behind the third. Cut off the end. Now work stake 2 in the same way and go round until all the stake ends have been woven in and cut off.

You can make a shallow basket or a deep basket by the length of the side stakes.

If you want to make a handle for a basket, cut a thick twig or shoot, wet it and then tie the ends together so that the twig is curved. Let it dry and then sharpen the ends. Push the ends down into the opposite sides of the basket and thread thin shoots through the basket, criss-crossing them over and over the handle ends to hold them firmly in position.

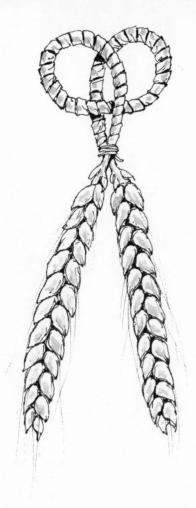

Corn weaving

You can weave corn to make pretty decorations called 'corn dollies'. The word 'dollies' probably comes from 'idols'. Thousands of years ago, figures or idols made from corn straw were part of pagan religious rites at harvest time. If you are interested in finding out more about this old, country craft, there are dozens of corn dolly patterns in craft books.

The easiest corn dolly is a simple two-straw design called the Lover's knot. Make one to decorate your bedroom wall as a reminder of your country holiday.

Lover's knot

You will need two long, ripe corn stalks with heads on them. Cut the stalks carefully from the very edge of the cornfield. Ask permission first if possible. Most farmers are very reasonable and will let you have a few straws of wheat if you are not greedy and behave in a responsible way. Strip the dried leaves from the stalks before you begin.

1 Tie the two straws together with a piece of thin twine or thread just under the heads.

2 Hold the straws in one hand, the heads downward and the ends apart. Number 1 is the straw on the right and number 2 is the straw on the left. Pick up straw 1 and fold it towards you over the tied knot. Flatten the fold with your thumb. Now pick up straw 2 and fold it towards you over straw number 1 and flatten the fold. Fold straw 1 away from you and over straw 2 and flatten the fold. Continue like this, folding one straw over the other and flattening each fold. The folding makes a thin braid.

3 Bend the finished braid into a loop like the illustration and tie the ends under the heads. Add a bow of ribbon if you like.

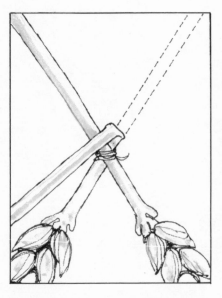

Natural dyeing

For thousands of years people dyed fabrics with
colours which they got from plants and fruits. The
colours were very soft and beautiful. Modern dyes
are made from chemicals. You can try the old way
of dyeing for yourself, using plants and fruits
collected on a country walk. Sheep wool takes
natural dyes best of all. See if you can find tufts of
sheep wool, caught on bushes and wire fences, to
experiment with.

Plants which make dye colours
A great many plants and flowers will produce dye
colour. Here are just a few of them and the colours
they will make.

Mountain laurel leaves, hickory tree bark, larch
needles, acorns, hop stalks, hawthorn berries, pine
cones and rowan berries will all make **brown** dye
colours.

Spinach leaves, gorse, silver birch bark, onion
skins, tansy flowers are just a few which will
produce **yellow.**

Beetroot, elderberries, wild plum tree bark,
hemlock tree bark, pokeweed and prickly-pear
cactus make **red** dyes.

Blackberries, sloe fruits, huckleberries and
bilberries will make **purple.**

Bracken tops, horsetail, nettles, carrot tops and
fern buds will make **green.**

Mahonia berries, parsley, bryony and some
mosses make **blue.**

Lichens, which are also a kind of plant produce
dye colours too. These are worth collecting because
they will dye fabric without your having to use a
mordant. Mordants are chemicals which are used
with natural dyes to make the colour brighter. They
also make the fabric take the colour better and 'fix'
the dye so that it does not wash out of the fabric

nor fade. There are several chemicals which are used as mordants. The most easily obtained is alum which can be bought from a chemist or druggist as a powder.

There are a few plants and fruits which you can use without mordants. These are onion skins, sloe berries, bilberries, golden rod flowers and of course, lichens.

Preparing lichens

Lichens are found growing in all kinds of places, on rocks, stone walls, on the bark of trees, on roof tiles and on wooden palings. There are a great many different types of lichen, and each of them produces different dye colours. When you are collecting, make sure you keep the different kinds separate.

Collecting lichen

Lichens are at their best towards the end of summer and just after rain. Scrape them up with a knife blade. Take them home and break up the pieces. Put a layer of lichen at the bottom of a pan. Put pieces of sheep wool on top and then another layer of lichen on top of the wool. Cover the lichens and wool with water. (Rain water is best but tap water will do just as well). Bring the pan slowly up to a boil and then simmer for about two hours. It is fascinating to see what colour comes out of the lichen. Keep a nature record of the colours that the different types of lichen produce.

Dyeing wools and fabrics

Only fabrics made of natural fibres will take natural dyes — wool, cotton and linen. Fabrics will not take dye colour if they have a crease resistent finish in them.

Useful addresses

Girl Guides Association
17-19 Buckingham Palace Road
London SW1

The Scout Association
25 Buckingham Palace Road
London SW1

The Camping Club of Great Britain and Ireland
      Limited
11 Lower Grosvenor Place
London SW1

Rough Stuff Fellowship
9 Matlock Road
Broadholme
Belper
Derbyshire (Cycle camping)

Young Explorer's Trust
238 Wellington Road South
Stockport

Youth Hostels Association
Trevalyn House
St Albans
Herts

Outward Bound Trust
14 Oxford Street
London W1

Other books you would enjoy reading

Walking, Hiking and Backpacking by Anthony
Greenbank, Constable

Survival for young people by Anthony Greenbank,
Piccolo

Bicycle Book by Richard Balantine, Piccolo

The Weather by F.C. Newing B.Sc. and Richard
Bowood, Ladybird

First Aid Junior Manual, British Red Cross
Society

Safety in Outdoor Pursuits, HMSO Department of
Education and Science

Observer's Book of the Weather by R.M. Lester,
Warne

Lightweight Camping, The Hike Book,
and *Camp and Trek* all by Jack Cox, Lutterworth
Press